Dear Mary Powell — I hope you enjoy reading this. Lots of love for Christmas — and hope to see you again soon (with the prospect of more carousing) —

Bertie
Christmas 1981

Letters to an Actress

Letters to an Actress

THE STORY OF IVAN TURGENEV AND MARYA GAVRILOVNA SAVINA

Translated and edited by
Nora Gottlieb and Raymond Chapman

Allison & Busby, London

First published in Great Britain 1973 by
Allison & Busby Limited, 6a Noel Street, London W1V 3RB

SBN 85031 104 7

© 1973 Nora Gottlieb and Raymond Chapman

PRINTED IN GREAT BRITAIN BY
THE ANCHOR PRESS LTD, AND BOUND BY
WM. BRENDON & SON LTD, BOTH OF TIPTREE, ESSEX

Contents

Introduction/7

LETTERS TO AN ACTRESS/25

Draft plan of Savina's Reminiscences/145

Principal Names mentioned in the text/147

Sources/151

References/153

Introduction

The old dotard married to a young wife is a perennial subject of comic satire: the elderly man who makes a fool of himself by trying unsuccessfully to possess a pretty girl is regarded with something like contempt. There is no place for satire or contempt in the love of Turgenev for the actress Marya Gavrilovna Savina. It brought him a sense of joy perhaps greater than he had ever known before, and it also stirred the sorrow of unfulfilled longing in the depths of his heart. But it never made him look or sound foolish, because he loved without losing respect for his own dignity or for Savina's right to independent existence.

His letters to her were written over a period of some four years, from the time of their first meeting in 1879 when she was playing Verotchka in *A Month in the Country* in Petersburg, until just before his death at Bougival in 1883. The typical Turgenev mood pervades them all—gentle, ironical, eager for love that will respond to his own warmth. The story which they tell could be one of his own tales. It would be the tale of a man destined to be forever an unsuccessful lover, half-resigned to his lot yet never losing his delight in beauty and in art.

It is a one-sided story because most of Savina's version is missing. We know something of what she felt in the early days of their acquaintance: the first meeting, Turgenev at the theatre to see her act in his play, their reading together at a charity recital, a visit of Turgenev to her flat and a few comments to other people. Then, as the affair develops, as Turgenev's feelings become more explicit, Savina falls silent. Yet she wrote to him continually, as his own letters to her make plain—to Spasskoye, to Petersburg, to Bougival.... The fate of those letters remains a mystery. Did Pauline Viardot, who kept her hold over Turgenev for forty years, destroy them in a fit of jealousy after his death? Are they still lying at the bottom of a trunk in some French attic? Or did they find their way back to Savina, who then destroyed them? The last explanation is the most plausible, if we take into account her known reticence about her private life, her refusal to permit a single one of Turgenev's letters to her to be published during her lifetime despite the importunity of journalists and others, her persistent silence in the face of questions. Add to all this the fact that she was at one time thought to have destroyed Turgenev's letters. Batyushkov certainly thought it likely—"As to the famous Turgenev letters, it is possible that she has destroyed them. Once, when I asked her what she intended to do with these letters, Marya Gavrilovna replied, 'The world will have no need of them. The letters will die with me.' "

We will never know if she had the heart to destroy what the great man had written—except for one letter that may have revealed too much about their relationship. She did not trust herself with it, gave it to Koni for safekeeping, but eventually retrieved and destroyed it. Fortunately, Koni's secretary Ponomarova had taken a copy and it can be printed.

A. F. Koni (1844–1927) plays so important a part in the relationship between Turgenev and Savina that he should be more fully introduced to the reader. He was an outstanding jurist, a senator and man of letters, who numbered among his friends Tolstoy, Goncharov and Dostoyevsky as well as

Turgenev and Savina. It was he who supplied Tolstoy with the plot for the novel *Resurrection*, which was based on one of his court cases. He is also famous for having succeeded in swaying the jury in favour of the woman revolutionary Vera Zasulich, for whom the Tsar and the Minister of Justice had demanded if not the death sentence then hard labour in Siberia. Koni was a man of high principles and infinite kindness. "Koni is a virtuoso at doing good," a friend had once said of him, "but while with others this beneficence is boring and banal, Koni's virtue is attractive, witty and alluring like vice."

With the coming of the Revolution, Koni lost his high position and his honours, but this did not seem to worry him. At the age of seventy-five, sick and hardly able to walk, he dragged himself all over Petrograd to give lectures to soldiers of the Red Army and to workers. For a lecture lasting two hours in starving Petrograd he would get as a fee a miserable herring. His listeners were deeply appreciative and in 1921 on his birthday they presented him with some white bread, an unheard-of luxury in those days. That he was not only a man of wide culture, of exceptionally lucid and imaginative mind, but also a great humanitarian, will appear from his sympathetic role in our story.

Certainly Savina did not wear her heart upon her sleeve, not only in her relationship with Turgenev. Her papers, many of which are still unpublished, contain a fair amount of valuable material about the theatre and society of her time but very little about her personal life. She seems indeed to have made a deliberate effort not to leave any record of her friendship with some of her outstanding male contemporaries; it is rumoured that she burned the letters which Goncharov wrote to her. Perhaps she dreaded the assumptions that would be made about Turgenev and herself if the relationship was widely known. She wrote to Koni in 1909: "The talent of a writer, of an artist, is the rightful property of the public; but they want everything served up. Under the pretence of 'extraordinary interest' they dissect one's soul—in most cases with a dirty knife."

It is clear from Turgenev's letters to Savina that he wished for the affair to develop into complete physical intimacy. "If only ... if only ..." runs like a refrain through his letters. Yet, for all her affection for Turgenev, which indeed amounted to something like veneration, Savina held back. She probably was unwilling to become too deeply involved with a man thirty-six years older than herself. In addition, for the whole period of the correspondence she was in love with Vsevolozhsky, whom she married in 1882, and there were other flirtations in the background. Yet some of her comments to her friends suggest more complex reasons. "I was a stupid girl. I simply could not understand how 'our famous man' could be attracted to me", she wrote to Filosofov; and in 1892 to Bazilevsky, "I have something contradictory in my nature. You know, I did not believe Ivan Sergeyevich—I mean, I was doubtful ..."

Savina may have known intuitively that it was wiser to let Turgenev keep his dream than to test and perhaps destroy it by the impact of reality. Only in the world of dreams could their friendship remain unscathed. "Stupid girl" though she called herself, she had the sense to make something of Turgenev's complex character. She accepted his own belief, once expressed in a letter to her, that it was best that "dreams should remain merely dreams". She herself suffered the tension between strong personality and creative talent, set against a deep humility and self-doubt. She was never sure that she would be able to live up to Turgenev's image of her. She accepted the opinion of Turgenev's friend the poet Polonsky as a "true interpretation", on an aspect of Turgenev's nature that is very germane to her relationship with him. The significant passage in Polonsky's appraisal is this:

As I understand it, Ivan Sergeyevich would never have been happy if he had married. A woman would make him lose interest in her if she did not know how to conceal from him the ordinary, prosaic side of her existence, or that trace of triviality which is not alien even to the great. Her very presence would become intolerable to him.

Yet the link that held Turgenev and Savina together was strong. She was, first and foremost, a great artist—a fact which was true also of Pauline Viardot, the celebrated opera singer to whom Turgenev kept returning and in whose home he died. He of all men would have understood what Savina meant when she wrote to an unknown correspondent in 1891:

> The stage is my life, or rather my poison. I was poisoned by the stage. If I were not to "die" on the stage at least once a month, I should die in reality. I cannot live "artificially" on the stage. I nearly always feel acutely on the stage: and when I am playing a favourite role of mine, it is as if I were performing a religious rite, I never think about my health. I have often arrived at the theatre very ill and recovered the moment I appeared before the public.

Savina was not conventionally beautiful, yet she was fascinating. Something of her attraction for men is expressed in a letter which Bazilevsky wrote to her in 1901:

> I will tell you something that probably few will tell you in this prim, deceitful Petersburg: when I read in the papers about the theatre, about art and new plays, about new trends, I see before me the figure of a slim, pert young woman, playful as a doe. This young woman is the Savina of the eighties. The lovely black eyes rivet the attention of the whole public, while the sensitive, passionate acting reminds one of the friskiness, the step and the nervous quivering of an Arab steed which, even while resting, is all movement. Yes, this Savina was brimful of life.

Her theatrical life spanned the years from the last works of Turgenev, Goncharov and Dostoyevsky down to the emergence of Meyerhold and Stanislavsky. She acted at the Alexandrinsky Theatre in Petersburg for forty years: for the theatre-going public of those years, Savina and the Alexandrinsky were almost synonymous. She raised the prestige of the theatre and of the acting profession by her introduction of new plays by contemporary writers and by the maintenance of a classical repertory in the face of the popular preference for vaudeville and operetta. There were many talented actors and actresses in Russia, some of the same stature as Savina, but the theatre as a great cultural and national institution was developing slowly. Her particular achievement was to help greatly in this development by continually introducing truly national and original plays as well as outstanding contemporary foreign plays which have since become classics.

The first theatre in Russia was built by Peter the Great, but there was a lack of plays and so this theatre languished. Only under Elisabeth, Peter's daughter, did a more serious interest in the theatre appear. A certain Volkov, son of a merchant, produced popular plays in Yaroslavl in 1750. Elisabeth called him and his company to Petersburg, where a permanent theatre was established in 1756—the first Imperial theatre, with others to follow in a number of places. Later on there were several private theatres, mostly on the estates of rich landowners, with their serfs as actors. In later years the repertory came to consist of translations of Shakespeare, Racine, Molière and of adaptations of other foreign plays. But it was the French vaudevilles and melodramas that dominated the Russian stage; they were the favourites of the Russian public, but could hardly develop the public's taste.

With Fonvizin's *The Minor* the national comedy was born in 1782. This comedy and Griboyedov's *Woe from Wit* (1833) were milestones on the road towards an original Russian theatre, followed by Gogol's *The Government Inspector* (1836), the plays by Ostrovsky and so towards the great Chekhov plays. The Russian theatre had come of age; it now needed a discriminating public, it needed prestige and recognition of the role that the actor played in the cultural life of the nation. By putting Russian plays on the stage, by dramatizing the great contemporary novels, by introducing significant foreign plays, an inspiring attempt was made to create a favourable climate for a highly artistic and energetic theatre life in Russia. In all this Savina, especially in her later years, played a leading part. She acted Katherina in *The Taming of the Shrew*; she played in Molière, in Lope da Vega, in Gogol's *The Government Inspector*; she was Nastasya Philippovna in the first dramatized version of *The Idiot*, and Akulina in Tolstoy's *The Power of Darkness*; she firmly established Turgenev's reputation as a dramatist on the Russian stage, and she sustained the waning reputation of the ageing Goncharov; she delighted Chekhov by agreeing to play Masha in *Ivanov*; she helped to introduce the work of Ibsen and was the first Russian actress to play Nora in *A Doll's House*.

The more she established herself as an actress, the more the spheres of literature and the theatre tended to overlap for her. When she was considering a play for production, she had no hesitation about expanding the size and importance of her own part if she thought it necessary—even when this was not the author's original intention. Often her emphasis proved to be the right one. Turgenev made no objection when she focused attention on Verotchka in *A Month in the Country*, instead of on the principal heroine, Natalya Petrovna. This part finally established her reputation as an actress and began her friendship with Turgenev.

It is not surprising that a woman like Savina should number among her friends some of the outstanding men of the time: Goncharov, Ostrovsky, Koni, and of course Turgenev.

Goncharov was devoted to her for years, right up to his death. When he gave her a copy of *The Same Old Story*, he wrote in it the inscription, "To a glorious actress, a delightful woman, and a dear good friend—to Marya Gavrilovna Savina—a tribute from an old man, the author, so that she may remember him with kindness".

Even Tolstoy fell under her spell, after a meeting which also reveals her talent for getting the most out of dramatic reading:

> Savina came to see me to ask permission to produce *The Power of Darkness*. But she is most anxious to play the part of Anyutka. Well, it seems that here I have upset her: I found that this role did not suit her, nor did that of Akulina ... I suggested to her that if she insisted on playing *either* of these parts it would be better to play that of Akulina, which seems more in her line although *she* says that it would not suit her. She listened modestly to everything I had to say and asked me to read aloud two scenes, which she herself then read; and, you know, she did not read at all badly. I had not expected that it would be so good. She had caught the right tone ... Yes, I suppose she is a clever girl, and quick ...

After she had gone, at supper Tolstoy was remorseful about having scoffed at Turgenev's passion for "the little actress". "You know, it's a good thing that I'm old," he kept on saying to his wife. "She is delightful—the way she read Anyutka! She is a clever girl through and through."

Between rehearsals and her evenings at the theatre, Savina found time to attend concerts, including those of new compositions by Tchaikovsky, and to visit exhibitions. She was an artist of wide culture. "It is my friends who teach me most," she used to say. In fact, she was self-taught, and she recalled the hard road which she had to travel to reach the artistic heights in her brief memoir *My Wanderings and Tribulations*.

When Turgenev lay dying at Bougival in 1883, she fulfilled the promise which she had made to him some time previously: that she would write about her life. Far away in the solitude of Siva, the estate of her second husband Vsevolozhsky, she brought the story from her childhood, through the beginning of her career as an actress, up to the season of 1876–7, two years before her first meeting with Turgenev. She meant to carry on with her autobiography and sketched the rough plan which is printed at the end of this book, but she never returned to writing. The slender volume that was published remains our chief source of information about her early life.

Savina began acting at the age of thirteen when she was thrust on to the stage by her disagreeable parents—actors themselves, though very inferior ones. Her father had been a teacher of calligraphy and drawing in Kamenets-Podolsk, where Savina was born in 1854. A certain success in amateur theatricals emboldened him to fancy his chances as a professional, so that he threw up his job, changed his name from Podramentsov to Stremlyanov—which has a more grandiloquent sound in Russian—and set off to tour provincial Russia with his wife and children. There were constant quarrels and scenes between the parents until eventually they separated. The mother, an unstable and hysterical woman who was continually involved in petty intrigues, preferred her second daughter Yelena to Savina. The latter, who had been subjected to daily insults and humiliations by the mother, stayed with her father until she won some measure of independence. She had not been allowed to finish school or been given any dramatic training.

Savina's "Academy of Drama" was situated among the various companies performing in provincial towns, from which she picked up technique and knowledge wherever she could. It was a hard school, with the jealousies and scheming of fellow-actors fighting for parts in the superficial and often vulgar vaudevilles and operettas that made up the repertoire. Savina learned how to make most of her stage clothes herself as the result of struggling to maintain her wardrobe on a meagre salary, and how to deal with the boorish managers of the companies. At the age of sixteen in 1870 she married the actor Savin, a petty-minded man of slight talent, addicted to drinking bouts and affairs with women. He led her a wretched life until she fled from him to Petersburg and finally got a divorce.

In spite of everything, Savina managed to learn her craft in those tempestuous provincial years. She had the intuition of a true artist and it taught her to discriminate and to discipline herself. There was talent as well as mediocrity in the companies. At the age of fifteen she had the good fortune to meet, in Minsk, two really accomplished actresses. One was Sandunova-Koni, formerly of the Imperial Theatre and the mother of Savina's lifelong friend A. F. Koni; the other was Shubert. Their influence on her was decisive: fortunately she was quick to learn.

Appointment to the Alexandrinsky Theatre in Petersburg was another uphill struggle, in which good luck, talent and determination played their part. Her ability had already made itself plain, and she was surprised to find that the standard of acting at the Alexandrinsky was not high and that the theatre itself was at a low ebb of fortune. It was indeed Savina's success that began its prosperity. Savina's mother and sister descended on her as soon as her position was established and the reports of her enthusiastic reception by the audience became known. They invaded her little flat in Petersburg and settled down there to look out for a part for Yelena. At her mother's instigation, Yelena went behind Savina's back to the director of the company and asked him for a part. Savina recalled the shock of that occasion years later:

"But all the parts have already been allocated," I exclaimed in astonishment when I saw my sister all dressed up for her visit to the director. "What kind of role do you expect to get?" "I hope to get Savina's parts," Yelena replied, while a wicked smile twisted her lips. "What will you do with Savina then?" I asked again. "You'll be thrown out as soon as I start acting."

Despite her natural outrage at this devious behaviour, the pain of which lingered for many years, Savina did not turn against her mother and sister when they fell on hard times. She looked after her mother, who eventually survived her, and maintained her in comfort; when Yelena died, Savina cared for her sons. She paid for her own brother's education to which no one else was giving a thought: her father seemed to have forgotten the boy's existence and her mother was penniless. It was Savina's fate to be exploited by those close to her. Her second husband, the flamboyant and aristocratic Vsevolozhsky, brought bankruptcy on himself and on her so that she was hounded by creditors and for a long time part of her salary went straight to pay his debts. It was only in her third marriage, to Molchanov, the vice-president of the Theatre Society, that she found true companionship and peace.

When Turgenev met Savina in the winter of 1879 and saw her acting in *A Month in the Country*, he was in a happy mood and in high spirits. He had met with an enthusiastic reception from the Russian public: a great reconciliation after years of misunderstanding and adverse criticism. Having been acclaimed at one time by a great section of the progressive intelligentsia as a champion of the people by reason of his *A Sportsman's Sketches* in 1852, he was then called an outright reactionary by the same group and accused of slandering the younger generation when *Fathers and Sons* appeared in 1862. The principal cause of this volte-face within a decade was the portrayal of the character Bazarov in the latter work. Bazarov is the dynamic "new man" of the age, the radical intellectual working for a break from the old ways. Turgenev himself had an ambivalent attitude to all that Bazarov represented. As a liberal, a man of the "forties", he supported movements for the abolition of serfdom and the establishment of the right to free speech. He even shared some of the contempt for members of his own class. At the same time he recoiled from the utilitarian view of art and the studied brusqueness which characterized the Bazarovs of real life. He could therefore admire without complete approval, could sympathetically understand the social conditions which had given birth to the new type, without completely identifying with the Bazarovs of his time.

As is the fate of those who see both sides in an inflammatory situation, Turgenev was attacked on apparently contradictory grounds. The ruling class called *A Sportsman's Sketches* "un livre incendiaire" and later reproached him for wooing the Nihilists, but approved his apparent exposure of the same party in *Fathers and Sons* to suit their own purpose. The political situation in those years was tense, with unrest among the intellectuals, with rioting and arson in Petersburg, with passionate arguments raging among writers and thinkers. Bazarov represented a new type of intellectual: no longer the cultivated aristocrat but the *raznochinets* of humbler origin, radical in politics and aesthetics alike. The new direction was represented in the development of the *Contemporary Review* which Turgenev, a contributor from its inception, had once affectionately called "our journal". Now he found himself increasingly at odds with the way it was tending. Despite his former close friendship with its editors, a series of disagreements and quarrels between 1858 and 1861 ended with a complete breaking-off of his connection with the journal.

By 1879, however, there had been changes in the political climate and the interpretation of Bazarov could be made with more understanding and detachment. He no longer seemed a caricature; his creation was vindicated by current social and intellectual developments. Turgenev had portrayed him ahead of his time, but now time had caught up with his portrayal. The public could once more see Turgenev as the man who had written *A Sportsman's Sketches* and he was given a tumultuous welcome. He was greeted with applause, toasted and honoured, almost carried shoulder-high by the students in Moscow and Petersburg, and he was intensely happy. Although his tendency to melancholy and weary resignation was not apparent just then, some understanding of his character and his previous life is necessary in order to explain why he was so quickly attracted to Savina and why the note of sadness creeps so often into his letters to her. There was in him an element of mildness amounting to weakness which affected his personal relationships. Yet, when principles were involved, he could be stubborn and uncompromising. The explanation must be sought in his early years and his family background.

Turgenev's father was a member of an old aristocratic family which had come down in the world. His mother was a wealthy heiress who owned vast estates but who was plain and older than her husband. The marriage was the result of family pressure on the father, who himself regarded his wife with distaste and soon began to find his consolation elsewhere: not a difficult task for an elegant, handsome young aristocrat in the Russia of that time. He took no interest in either the estates or the children of his marriage but left everything to his autocratic and domineering wife. Turgenev himself adored his father and was wounded by the coldness and remoteness that he encountered.

Turgenev's short novel *First Love* (1860) is a key to his relationship with his father, and hinges on an event that had a shattering effect on him in 1831. "This is life itself," he said of this book, "this is no invention. When I read it, I get a whiff of the past." Although it is a slight piece of work, it is as vital a key to Turgenev as *David Copperfield* is to Dickens. The boy in the story is sixteen: Turgenev himself was three years younger. He loves, with the pure adoration of a young boy, the attractive, wilful and capricious Zinaida who is in her early twenties. The traumatic experience that shatters him is the discovery that Zinaida has become his father's mistress and has changed into a gentle, serious and submissive young woman. The playful condescension with which she has treated the boy, as a princess might treat her page, is gone for ever. "I cannot love those on whom I have to look down," she used to say, "I need a man who can break my will . . . I love the man who is my master."

"Is this love?" the boy asks when he learns the truth. "Yes, this is love, this passion is love", he decides. The discovery shakes him to the heart. "All my flowers were torn up by their roots, scattered around me and crushed." Love seemed like a cruel game, a disease; and at last the father, dying, writes to him, "My son, beware of a woman's love—fear this happiness like poison."

There was no compensating love for Turgenev from his mother, tyrannical and with a lust for power, careless of other people's feelings. She left an indelible mark on him and her character is drawn in his story *Mumu*. At first she spoiled him and treated him as her favourite, and he did all that his affectionate, sensitive nature could to please her. But her savagery towards her servants and serfs revolted him and, despite his meekness in other ways, made him oppose her until the break between them came. He accepted the material consequences of the estrangement; his mother withdrew all financial support and left him to his own resources. The emotional consequences were not so easily borne; her ruthless will had crushed his own will and undermined his self-confidence. He once admitted to having "little respect for my own identity" and he never found it easy to set his own will firmly against that of another person.

The effect on his relations with women was, predictably, to leave him sadly resigned to a life without full satisfaction; he was, continually, the unsuccessful lover. He once said to Savina at his country estate Spasskoye, referring to a character in *A Month in the Country*, "Rakitin is myself—I have always been the unsuccessful lover." Yet he longed for love and felt his life starved of some essential quality. He never married but had to cling to someone else's "nest", as he put it, instead of having one of his own. Establishing no family for himself, he accepted admission into another family with mingled happiness and resignation.

The family that acted as a substitute for his own was that of Pauline Viardot, whom he met when she was appearing in Petersburg in 1843. She was then and for many years afterwards the most highly acclaimed singer in Europe, admired by famous writers and musicians for her magnificent voice and great artistry, combined with a strong, fiery temperament which cast her in the traditional image of a prima donna. She was born in Paris in 1821 and died there in 1910, but came from an artistic Spanish family named Garcia; both her father and her brother were singers. She counted among her friends some of the most outstanding people of her time, including George Sand and the composer Gounod. She corresponded with Dickens and she was admired by Chopin, Tchaikovsky and Heine. Her drawing-room was a centre of artistic life. Turgenev's love for her grew into a consuming passion which lasted for forty years, though it was waning in the last period of his life when he knew Savina. For Turgenev art was a focal point of life; his friend the poet Polonsky once remarked that Turgenev was an artist to the marrow of his bones. A woman, a singer, an artist like Viardot brought him to her feet. It was the artist as much as the woman that kept him under her spell for so long. Polonsky could understand how she attracted the great writer:

Just as actresses playing the part of Lady Macbeth, or Ophelia, or a Parisian Camelia, or simply a chatty gossip, could arouse the spectator's admiration by their perfect acting—so Mme Viardot seems to have had the talent to act divinely and appear to anyone just as she wished to appear, not only on the stage of the theatre but also on the stage of life. Turgenev with his particular bent of mind and character, could not help admiring such a woman—of whom there are few.

Even in her old age she could charm people. When Tchaikovsky visited her in Paris in 1886 he wrote: "Of all my new acquaintances, it was Mme Viardot who made the most enchanting impression on me. This old lady of seventy is full of energy, brimming with life, interested in everything, knows everything, and is extremely charming." And to Mme von Meck he wrote, "As to the question whether Viardot remembers Turgenev, I must tell you that she not only remembered him but that nearly all the time we spoke only of him; she told me in detail how they wrote together the *Song of Triumphant Love*." Viardot was in fact rather given to boasting about her contribution to Turgenev's work, although in this instance the power of her music had had its effect on his words.

It generally happens when a woman has exerted strong influence over the life of a famous man that people will take sides in a controversy over whether the influence was detrimental or beneficial. In this case there were many, particularly in Russia, who detested Pauline Viardot for keeping Turgenev away from his homeland. Whatever the rights of the matter may be—and they are too complex to unravel here—there is no doubt that Turgenev worshipped her. "If I were a tree, you would be my crown and my roots", he wrote to her. She accepted him for a short time as her lover, and then treated him as a friend of the family until his death. Turgenev was on good terms with her husband Louis Viardot: the strange *ménage à trois* followed a seeminly calm existence. Turgenev shared in the joys and sorrows of the Viardots and persuaded himself that he indeed had his family—"My only family" he called it. He once declared, "If the Viardot family were to emigrate to Australia I would go with them." No errand that he could undertake for any member of the family seemed too trivial for him. And yet, despite the illusory security of this way of life, he knew in his heart that he was essentially a lonely man. There were times when the relationship with Pauline Viardot was at a low ebb, and he would turn to other women, as his letters to Baroness Lambert and Countess Vrevskaya reveal.

By the time he met Savina, what remained of Turgenev's passion for Viardot was a calm friendship, coupled with the realization of loneliness. A comparison of the letters to Viardot and to Savina shows a striking similarity between some images and expressions. When he speaks of a release of emotion and hopes for a reciprocation, he uses to Viardot the image of a dam that is breached ("Maintenant que la digue est rompu..."), and to Savina of a bolt pushed back ("Avez-vous fermé—ou bien ouvert—le verrou?"). A line from Gogol's *Notes of a Madman* occurs again and again in his letters to both women— "Never mind, let us keep silent." He uses it to calm his heart when he writes to Savina and, slightly altered, in telling Viardot of the whirl of events—"Two more weeks, and I shall be racing to Moscow, to Petersburg, to Berlin, to Baden! Never mind, never mind, calmness above all!"

Another recurring feature of his correspondence is the preoccupation with women's hands, which seemed strangely to have fascinated him. The endless kissing of hands verbalized in his letters both to Viardot and to Savina goes beyond the polite custom of contemporary society. He kisses their hands—lingeringly—tenderly—he writes that their hands are beautiful, dear, intelligent, fascinating. His dislike of clumsy hands comes out in a letter from Karlsbad to Pauline Viardot's daughter Claudie—a particular favourite of his whom he knew as "Didi". He sends her a drawing of the hotel chambermaid, a caricature reminiscent of the style of Wilhelm Busch, in which her thick red hands are prominent. "I assure you," he writes, "if you had hands like these I should not kiss them so often." To Savina he writes, "And so be sure to write—and soon, otherwise I shall be cross with you and not want to kiss your hands, even in my imagination. No, nonsense—I shall always want to kiss them, and not only them, but..." He once asked Savina to send him a cast of her hand.

Turgenev and Savina both suffered more from the lack of parental love in their early years than falls to the lot of most people. It is not surprising that a note of sadness and dissatisfaction ran through both lives and shadowed the success of accomplished art. Exactly how much each of them gained from their few years of friendship could probably never be communicated in words. But Turgenev's letters tell a story that must stand with some of the great records of human loving. Let them speak now for themselves.

NORA GOTTLIEB

Letters to an Actress

[Savina tells how she came to know Turgenev.]*

A Month in the Country[1] was first produced in Petersburg on 29 January 1879, for my benefit performance. It took me a long time to find a suitable play, especially as I was looking for something "literary", and finally I came upon Turgenev's comedy quite by chance. It had never been performed in Petersburg but it undoubtedly deserved a production. I liked the part of Verotchka—although it was not the principal one—but the play as it stood seemed to me boring and too long. All the same, I made up my mind to get it produced. I discussed the play with my fellow-actors and met some disagreeable responses. For instance Nilsky, the *jeune premier* at that time, categorically refused to play the part of Rakitin which he considered too poor for him. Sazonov was not keen on the part of the husband—and every part brought similar reactions from the company.

In addition, Sazonov shared my feelings about weaknesses in the play itself and advised me to consult Krylov about some cuts. I agreed to this, provided we first asked the author's permission. So this play brought about my friendship with

---

*Editorial commentary and explanations are in square brackets throughout.

Turgenev. He was living in Paris at the time, and I wired to ask his permission for cutting—production without permission would have been unthinkable. He wired back, "Agreed but regretfully, as the play was not intended for the stage and is unworthy of your talent." Since Turgenev had no knowledge of my "talent" this was only a formal courtesy.

[Turgenev, however, was seriously concerned about the proposal; on 23 January 1879 he wrote from Paris to his friend and agent Toporov: "... Last night I received a telegram from M. G. Savina, the actress, asking permission for some cuts in my comedy *A Month in the Country*, which she has chosen for her benefit performance on 29 January. I can't think what made her choose such a theatrically impossible play! One Moscow actress—Vasilyeva—attempted it a few years ago in spite of my repeated warnings and was an utter flop. The same thing is in store for Mme Savina. Of course I wired that I will let her make any cuts that she wishes; but, not knowing her private address, I sent the wire to the Alexandrinsky theatre. When you receive this letter, please go and see her for me—you won't have any difficulty in finding out where she lives—and repeat my permission in case the telegram hasn't reached her for any reason. You could also tell her how anxious and troubled I am—by the way, I said as much in my telegram."

Turgenev need not have worried; both the play and Savina were received with enthusiasm.]

The play was produced, and it created a sensation. I had great success in my role as Verotchka, which became my favourite part—my "creation". I gave myself up entirely to the role. I did not *play* Verotchka—I performed a sacred rite—I walked in the clouds. That night, there was an electric current between myself and the audience. I felt that they loved me, loved Verotchka for my complete identification with her. They called repeatedly for the author, as I wired next day to tell him.

Turgenev replied, "Mille remerciements pour attention délicate, compliments du succès rendu possible par votre talent. Attribute success to your wonderful talent and hope very soon to thank you in person."

He did indeed come to Russia soon afterwards and was received with great enthusiasm. He made his appearance in Petersburg like a being descended from the sky. A few days before his arrival, a certain Toporov—a friend of his who managed his affairs—came to see me and asked in the course of conversation whether I intended to go and see Ivan Sergeyevich. Somehow I had not thought this possible, that is to say, I had not thought of it at all. Perhaps I might meet him some time at the theatre (after all, he would surely be curious to see his play on the stage) at a suitable opportunity... But Toporov declared that Ivan Sergeyevich wished to meet me and had suggested fixing a time for the second day after his arrival and letting him know.

As this "hour" approached, I suffered such an attack of nerves that I almost decided not to go and—ran down the stairs calling to the coachman in a choking voice, "To the Hotel Europa."

I do not remember how I climbed the hotel stairs, how I was shown the room. I remember only how at the very door I came upon Toporov and saw him as my good angel.

"Go straight in," he said. "Ivan Sergeyevich is eagerly awaiting you."

When we entered, a visitor was just getting up to take his leave, and Ivan Sergeyevich came towards me with outstretched hands. His giant figure emanated something so warm and familiar, this was such a lovable, elegant "grandpa", that I immediately felt at ease and, forgetting my fear of "Turgenev", began talking to him as to an ordinary mortal.

"I never thought you were so young! I had imagined you quite different. You do not look at all like an actress!"

Naturally I invited him to come to the theatre to see *A Month in the Country*. But here a misunderstanding appeared; for some reason he had supposed that I was playing the part of Natalya Petrovna—the principal part—and had completely forgotten about Verotchka.

"True, you are too young for the part of Natalya Petrovna, but Verotchka ... what is there to play?" he kept on repeating in a puzzled manner.

He was obviously grieved. I started to describe to him what a magnificent performance Varlamov had given of Bolshintsev and to give a general account of the way the play had been performed on the first night. He had no idea what our company was like and the only one he knew slightly was Abarinova who was playing the part of Natalya Petrovna—and this only thanks to the fact that she had taken lessons with Mme Viardot once upon a time.

I stayed for a quarter of an hour and left in a daze. As I went downstairs I continued to see the grey head of Ivan Sergeyevich as he bent over the banister and his friendly parting gesture and heard him say to Toporov, "She is quite charming, and evidently a clever girl."

At the time, I was twenty-five. I had so often heard people calling me "charming" that eventually I had come to believe it myself, but to hear Turgenev call me "a clever girl" ... this was happiness of a kind which even now it is hard to believe. I flew downstairs blushing with delight, but stopped on the last step as if thunderstruck.

"I never said anything about his writing!! There's a clever girl for you!"

This thought completely spoiled the impression of my visit to him. I returned home in great distress.

Toporov had been present throughout the meeting, gazing

with reverent admiration at the old writer, never moving. He was like an ikon-lamp, ever burning before Turgenev. An hour after my return, he arrived to tell me of the impression I had made on Ivan Sergeyevich.

"He particularly liked the fact that you never mentioned his writing," said Toporov. "It is so trite and bores him when people do."

I burst out laughing and described to him how scared I had been about the omission. We went on laughing about this episode for a long time.

[From what she told Belyayev about this meeting, Savina left most of the talking to Turgenev and was not so voluble as her reminiscences suggest. However, she showed no lack of resource when Turgenev was to attend a performance of *A Month in the Country* on 27 March.]

"You've invited Ivan Sergeyevich to come and watch his play, but where are you going to seat him?" Toporov asked me. "Every ticket is sold, and besides he cannot appear among the audience. It would mean an endless ovation and he would see nothing of the play."

It seemed to be an extremely difficult situation, but kind Toporov himself thought of a solution—the director's box!

Nothing better could be imagined and the very next day I went to Lukashevich, the repertory manager, to suggest offering the director's box to the author, especially as all the seats in the theatre had been sold long ago. Lukashevich, a stickler for formality and a typical bureaucrat from top to toe, was nonplussed by my suggestion and said that it was quite impossible to make a decision without the Baron. (Baron Kister was at that time the director of all the Imperial theatres.) He could not see his way to approaching the Baron with this request.

"You write in your own name and I will send the letter by

messenger," he added. To write to the Baron, or to approach him on any excuse was at that time considered a heinous crime, but of course I did not hesitate for a minute. Lukashevich advised me to ask discreetly for "a seat in the box" and not for the whole box. In my liberal view this seemed almost insulting; but then, "clever girl" that I was, I realized that such a reaction was silly and I followed his advice. Within an hour the messenger returned with a ticket and a letter from the Baron, permitting me to place his box at the disposal of the "venerable author".

At five o'clock on the day of the performance I personally took the ticket around to Ivan Sergeyevich. I did not go in but left it with my visiting card.

I cannot describe how tremulously I waited for the evening and how I acted; this was one of the happiest performances of my life—perhaps the happiest. It was as though I were performing a sacred rite . . . I felt quite distinctly that Verotchka and I were one and the same person . . . I had no thought for what was going on in the audience!

During the whole of the first act Ivan Sergeyevich was hiding in the obscurity of the box, but during the second act the audience caught sight of him. Scarcely was the curtain lowered, when the cry of "Author" rose from all sides. In ecstasy, I rushed into the director's box and began to drag him unceremoniously by his sleeve towards the stage. I wanted so much to show him to all of them, especially as those sitting on the right of the auditorium could not yet have seen him. But Ivan Sergeyevich declared very firmly that by stepping on to the stage he would be presenting himself as a dramatic author—something of which he "had not dreamed in his wildest dreams". He would, therefore, bow from the box and in fact did so at once. He had to go on bowing right through the evening, for the audience was wild with enthusiasm. I could not help feeling proud of the success of the play, since it had not occurred to anyone to produce it before my decision...

After the third act (the famous scene between Verotchka and Natalya Petrovna) Ivan Sergeyevich came into my dressing-room, approached me with wide eyes, took both my hands in his and led me to the gas-light. Then, looking at me intently as if seeing me for the first time, he began to study my face and said "Verotchka... have I really written this Verotchka? I didn't even pay attention to her when I was writing... the focal point of the play is Natalya Petrovna... your Verotchka is alive... what great talent you have!"

On hearing these words, still feeling myself to be Verotchka, a girl of seventeen, I could not think of anything better than to run up to him, embrace and warmly kiss this dear, wonderful writer. My mother was standing there in tears from emotion and people were crowding in the doorway of my dressing-room in the hope of seeing Turgenev at close quarters. He repeated his words once more and, as he left, said again, "Is it really I who wrote this?"

I took him behind the scenes to introduce the rest of the cast to him. He thanked everyone, but he kissed Varlamov. Everyone went on the stage and the interval was prolonged, but the audience was patient: they knew that the actors were doing honour to the author. I was in such rapture that I seemed to be walking on air. Abarinova kept on saying, "I know him—don't forget I took lessons with Mme Viardot." ... However, this did nothing towards helping her understand the part of Natalya Petrovna, and Ivan Sergeyevich sadly admitted as much. Towards the end of the performance the ovations became tempestuous. When the author, tired of bowing, left the theatre, the audience kept on calling for the actors.

Later on, I came to realize why Turgenev paid little attention to Verotchka and considered Natalya Petrovna the most important character in the play. Such a Natalya Petrovna actually existed in real life. I have forgotten her surname, but when I was staying at Spasskoye Turgenev even showed me her portrait. And he added, "Rakitin is myself. I'm always the unsuccessful lover in my novels."

[Turgenev lost no time in calling on Savina the next day, having written her a note—"Dear Marya Gavrilovna, I shall come to your place today, at 4 o'clock sharp. Just now I must tell you that your talent is great—divine. I kiss both your hands with deep emotion, Yours, I.T."]

The kindly Toporov told me of the coming visit. I cannot begin to describe with what agitation I awaited it and how I prepared myself; but everything turned out quite differently from my expectation. Ivan Sergeyevich kept on scrutinizing me with great interest. He wanted to know how I became an actress, my views on art, my family circumstances. He said incidentally that my manner of acting reminded him of the famous French actress Dècle, who had died of consumption at the age of twenty-four, but she had lacked my spontaneity. It seemed to me that he regarded me as an odd little "monkey". I was a trifle nervous to begin with, but I felt instinctively that I had got him interested in me. I decided to say whatever came into my head at the time, especially since I sensed a certain surprise on his part as if he felt, "Well! So that is what you Russian actresses are like!" This touched me on the raw and stung my national pride, as well as making me feel hurt on his account.

My usual spontaneity made me forget my duties as a hostess, my shyness, the appropriate tact—with the result that I blurted out a diatribe against his Westernism and on behalf of Russian art, "in which he did not seem to be interested, defending the Russia forgotten by him!" When I had finished, I saw that he was leaning back in his chair, his pince-nez fallen from wide open eyes, making a helpless gesture with his hands. Toporov, who had come along with him, told me later that Ivan Sergeyevich took a long time to recover from my outburst and kept on recalling various phrases I had used.

"You have stung him with your reproaches, and a good thing too," Toporov said with delight. He adored Turgenev and was always dreaming of bringing him "home". He hated Mme Viardot with all his heart and never let pass an opportunity of saying something malicious about her (not, of course, in the presence of Ivan Sergeyevich).

[Turgenev and Savina met again that same evening. The famous littérateur Peter Isayevich Weinberg, always organizing recitals for the "Literary Fund", decided to take advantage of the rare presence of Turgenev in Petersburg. He devised a programme in which both Turgenev and Dostoyevsky were to take part: a popular attraction, but not a very wise one in view of the relations between the two writers and the partisan feelings which they aroused. Savina was also invited to read.]

I was very worried, since I did not know what to choose for my reading. Once again, dear Toporov helped me out of my difficulty by suggesting a scene from *The Provincial Lady*. I was delighted with this happy idea and thanked him from the bottom of my heart. When I announced my choice to the organizers they all approved, but suddenly one of them asked, "Will you be reading with the author?"

Indeed—with whom was I to read the dialogue? No idea about the author had occurred to me, and I was completely stunned. I felt that to read with the author would be intolerably presumptuous, and for some reason I was sure that Ivan Sergeyevich "would not wish it". P. I. Weinberg had also been suggested as my reading-partner and it was he who took it upon himself to talk the matter over with the author. Ivan

Sergeyevich began by making excuses, and made me laugh when he said that he was afraid of disgracing himself by comparison with an actress; eventually he agreed, "provided the rehearsal does not turn out too badly". So the posters announced: "A reading from *The Provincial Lady* by Turgenev, given by the author and M. G. Savina".

The appearance of Turgenev for the first part of the evening was greeted by an ovation and for some time he was unable to start reading. He read the story, "The Pessimist". On the whole Turgenev did not read very well, and to make matters worse he was nervous. Our item in the programme was to be in the second part of the evening. A table with two candles was brought on, two books were placed on the table, two chairs drawn up... and we had to appear. Even now, after so many years, my heart sinks at the mere memory—but at the time!... Ivan Sergeyevich took me by the hand, Weinberg gave the word, "You are on!" Applause started behind the scenes and was taken up by the audience and I, dazed and trembling, stepped on to the stage. When we came on, I naturally did not acknowledge the applause but myself clapped the author. Ivan Sergeyevich had to go on bowing for some time, but at last silence fell and we began with the opening words of the scene—"Are you paying a long visit to us, your Excellency?"

I had scarcely managed to say these words when the applause broke out again. Ivan Sergeyevich smiled. It seemed that the ovation would never stop, and I—feeling my responsibility as a "professional" actress—advised him to stand up, as he was looking at me in great confusion. At last the audience quietened down and he replied. An extraordinary silence fell over the hall. All the organizers—the littérateurs, and even Dostoyevsky who was taking part in the evening—went into the pit to listen. I had completely recovered from my nervousness, gradually got into the part and was apparently reading well. I cannot describe the ovation at the end of our reading. Ivan Sergeyevich was showered with laurels. We were called out countless times but after making two appearances before the audience—and those at the insistence of Ivan Sergeyevich—I hid in the wings behind the organizers and applauded with them.

Dostoyevsky came up to me in the dressing-room and said, "Every word of yours is like finely-carved ivory, but as for the old man—he lisps."

I was distressed by this praise which was inspired, so it seemed to me, by hostility to Ivan Sergeyevich. Or was it the atmosphere of the hall that made me inclined to think so?... The audience! I had always been amazed by the wish of the public to take sides. As if there can be any question of sides when giants like Dostoyevsky and Turgenev meet... This evening, incidentally, was marked by a small incident which typifies this kind of thing. When Dostoyevsky stepped on the platform, the applause became more intense: somebody wanted to prove something to somebody. One well-known lady led up to the platform her beautiful little daughter, who presented Dostoyevsky with a huge bouquet of roses and thus put him in a very awkward situation. With the bouquet of roses he cut a comic figure, and he could not fail to realize this as well as the fact that the bouquet was intended to even up the score of the ovations. It was tactless towards the guest in whose honour all had gathered, and also tactless towards Dostoyevsky, who had no need of a rival to win the audience's approval.

Not long before the arrival of Ivan Sergeyevich in Petersburg, I had taken part in a charity concert where I saw how the public worshipped Dostoyevsky's genius... He was a remarkable reader. How could this frail, thin figure sustain such power and volume? "Fire the hearts of the people with the word"—I can hear it now. This bouquet caused some confusion among the audience, but even greater ovations for both writers followed.

[That same evening, Turgenev gave Savina a photograph of his portrait, inscribed, "To Marya Gavrilovna Savina in memory of our joint reading. With sincere devotion, Ivan Turgenev." They must have met at least once more before Turgenev left Petersburg. On 29 March, the day following their first meeting and the literary readings, Turgenev wrote a note to Savina—"The two words dropped by you yesterday permit me to remind you that I shall be at home on *Monday* from 2–3.30. Avis à la lectrice. Yours, with sincere devotion, Ivan Turgenev."]

After the departure of Ivan Sergeyevich, a regular correspondence started between the two of us. He was interested in every new part that I was playing, became indignant over the choice of the repertoire, and often finished his letters by expressing regret that he was not a "playwright"—"*What* a part I should write for you!"

[The regular correspondence did not really begin for some time, and the friendship developed only after the second meeting and the frequent meetings which followed it. In the meantime Savina kept silent. But Turgenev's letters from Paris to friends in Russia, especially to Toporov, reveal the interest that Savina had aroused in him and the impression she had made on him. Henceforth, their relationship is preserved mainly in Turgenev's words. At first there are only stray phrases and sentences:]

(6 April 1879 to Toporov) Should you see Savina, kiss her little hands for me, which will undoubtedly give you pleasure too.[2]

(17 April 1879 to J. P. Polonsky) My warm greetings to all my friends, not forgetting Savina.[3]

(2 May 1879 to Toporov) I see in the papers that Savina is ill. I hope it is not serious. Give her my regards.[4]

(29 May 1879 to Toporov) With Savina it seems to be, out of sight, out of mind.[5]

(14 June 1879 to Toporov from Bougival) My compliments to the Samarskys and to Marya Gavrilovna Savina, and tell her I am very sorry that I shall not see her soon. If she permits you, kiss her little hand for me.[6]

(6 September 1879 to Toporov from Bougival) [He intends to spend the winter in Petersburg but has not fully decided and is anxious that his friends nearby—the Viardot family—shall not learn of it.] Tell Savina that I shall permit myself to reciprocate her kindness as soon as I arrive. She is very charming and I feel genuinely attracted to her.[7]

(26 September 1879 to Toporov from Bougival) Should you see Savina, tell her that in imagination I kiss her little hands.[8]

(3 October 1879 to Toporov) Tell Savina that no one will prevent her from giving me again what I will return to her.[9]

(24 October 1879 to Toporov) And tell dear Savina that now she has fresh claims on my gratitude. Be sure that I shall kiss her little hands to my heart's content when we meet![10]

[The last letter reveals that Turgenev had asked Savina to be of some help to Toporov and to give him an introduction to someone unspecified. The same matter is referred to in Turgenev's first direct letter to Savina before they met again.]

(8 November 1879)
Dear Marya Gavrilovna,

I hear from Toporov that you have expressed a wish for my photograph, and I hasten to fulfil a wish that flatters me so highly. At the same time, let me thank you from the bottom of my heart for everything that you have done for my friend. He is a good man, devoted to you and fully deserving your interest in him—you will never regret having recommended him, I assure you. In a month or so I shall have the great pleasure of seeing you again; for the moment, just stretch out your pretty little hands to me so that I may kiss them with the tender feeling (half fatherly, half different) which I have for you.

Your sincerely affectionate Ivan Turgenev.[11]

[Although Turgenev wrote to Savina on 13 February 1880 implying that he had just arrived in Petersburg, he had actually come four days earlier.]

Dear Marya Gavrilovna,

I arrived an hour ago and shall be very glad to see you. I cannot leave the house at present—on my way here at night I suffered an attack of gout in my foot—not as bad as all that. So should you decide to visit me tomorrow you are sure to find me at home! Yours, I. Turgenev. (next day) My foot is better and I can leave the house. I don't want you to call while I am out, so please let me know through the bearer of this note at what time you intend to visit me or when I may present myself at your place.

Yours, I. Turgenev.[12]

(19 February 1880)
Dear Marya Gavrilovna,

Since you, in the kindness of your heart, enquire after my health, I think it is my duty to report that it is improving; I already walk about the room—though with crutches—but I hope in a few days to pay "homage" to you personally. I hear that you too are getting better [Savina had been unwell and did not act from 29 January to 14 February] and will once again delight the audiences who are so much in love with you. Toporov has been unable to call on you in the past few days (it is through him that I get reliable reports about the state of your health) for he too has been ill.

In any case, I shall see you soon, but for the moment I kiss your pretty little hands and ask you not to forget your Ivan Turgenev.[13]

(three days later) I am a little better, but I still do not leave the house and cannot take a step without crutches. This is of little importance; but it is too bad that you are unwell. However, I am convinced that as soon as you step on to the stage once more you will blossom into life—that is why I welcome your trip to Moscow. It will be a great pleasure to see you tomorrow—for the time being I kiss your little hands and remain,

yours, Iv. Turgenev.[14]

(the same day)
Dear Marya Gavrilovna,
Your maid had scarcely left my house when I remembered that I had not written down Maslov's address for you. Here it is: His Excellency, Ivan Ilyitch Maslov, Moscow . . . He is crazy about you as it is, so if you write to him he will go completely off his head; a healthy thing to happen to old men. Until tomorrow, I hope.

Yours, Iv. Turgenev.[15]

(25 February 1880)
Dear Marya Gavrilovna,
The fact that I have not yet called on you is the surest proof that I am not allowed to leave the house; but I am better and may be allowed to go out tomorrow for the first time. Meanwhile I see that Nilsky's benefit performance has not been cancelled and that you are taking part in it. I am delighted, for this must mean that you have recovered. I am sure you

understand how anxious I am to be in the theatre to see you in your new part. Therefore I am turning to you with the request to get me a ticket in any row—even the first—and at any price. I very much hope that you will do what I ask—and meanwhile I want you to believe in the sincere attachment of your devoted Iv. Turgenev.[16]

(two days later)
Dear Marya Gavrilovna,
  One of my friends—A. N. Mukhortova—would love to get a box for the performance of *The Wild One*: the first box in the first circle if possible. I shall be coming with her, so don't bother to get a ticket in the stalls as you kindly promised but get the box instead. My thanks in advance, and I am very much looking forward to applauding you tonight. Keep well, and au revoir.
  Your devoted Iv. T.
  P.S. Am I right in expecting you at my place tomorrow at 2.30? I shall be at home. Perhaps majesty will relax a little.[17]

(26 March 1880)
Dear Marya Gavrilovna,
  If you really mean to do what you mentioned yesterday, please fix a day now for next week so that I can keep it free.
  I warmly shake your beautiful little hands; your devoted friend Iv. T.
  P.S. The 21st, 22nd and 23rd are already booked.[18]

(11 April 1880—Savina's birthday)
My dear Marya Gavrilovna,
  Toporov, who will bring this letter to you, will also tell you how sad I am at not being able to dine with you. I am worse, have a cough and no voice—and in this state I am supposed to read tonight! I shall probably be unfit to read,

but in any case I must not budge until the evening. You can imagine how unpleasant all this is to me.

Accept my sincerest congratulations, which cannot be delivered in person, and also the enclosed trinket which will, I hope, sometimes remind you of me. I kiss your pretty hands and remain, cordially,

your devoted Iv. T.[19]

[Savina wrote the word "bracelet" at the top of this letter. The bracelet which Turgenev sent her was of gold inscribed inside: "To Marya Gavrilovna Savina from Ivan Sergeyevich Turgenev". It is now in the Leningrad State Museum. Despite his cough, Turgenev managed to attend the Literary Evening which was arranged by the Literary Fund in the Assembly Rooms.]

(the same day)
Dear Marya Gavrilovna,

My good friend Alexandra Nikolayevna Mukhortova is going to call for me tonight and take me to the Noblemen's Assembly. If this is inconvenient for you, please drive straight to the Assembly. But I must tell you that Mukhortova is dying to meet you and that this acquaintance should bring you nothing but pleasure. I kiss your hands,

Yours, Iv. Turgenev.[20]

[Savina responded with a present for Turgenev, apparently something which she had personally embroidered.]

(14 April 1880)
Marya Gavrilovna,

What a delightful present! I kiss in gratitude the pretty hands that have toiled over it. Your messenger told me that you will not be able to visit me today—yet you write in your note that you will be here at 2 o'clock. Anyway, I shall be at home until 4 o'clock—I may, possibly, leave the house for the first time today. Mukhortova—you have turned her head too—tells me that she means to invite you to her house for tea on Saturday. Do come—you will be so welcome. I shall be there as well. However, I shall see you before then. Once more my thanks, and I kiss your hands again.

Your friend I.T.[21]

[Savina accepted Mukhortova's invitation; in the draft for her Reminiscences she notes, "Evening at her house". Turgenev's growing regard for Savina was not received quite as he would have liked. He left Petersburg on 29 April, having written to her on the previous day:]

Dear Marya Gavrilovna,

This is to let you know that I have the doctor's permission to travel tomorrow night. There have recently been all kinds of "diplomatic subtleties and ambiguities" between us, and I want us to part as friends. Won't you have a cup of tea with me at my place tonight? We should chat as of old—like friends—and say good-bye until next winter, or next year. Drop me a line in reply.

Your sincerely devoted Iv. Turgenev.[22]

(Moscow, 30 April 1880)

I arrived here this morning, and now in the evening I wanted to send you a line. Although I asked you not to come to the station, to avoid any fuss when I left, yet I was sorry that I did not see your face once more. Of all the memories of Petersburg, the dearest and best are of you. Do write me a few words about your plans: I shall be staying here until next Saturday. And let me know how your part in the new play is going. The whole stretch of country between Petersburg and Moscow is snowbound as if it were December; yet Moscow is flooded and there is slush everywhere.... This spring is not a very beautiful one.

My health has improved completely: I hope that you too are fit and well. I'm somewhat depressed; well, that should pass soon.

I kiss your pretty hands and ask you to believe in the sincere friendship of
your devoted Iv. Turgenev.[23]

(Moscow, 6 May 1880)
Dear Marya Gavrilovna,

Late last night I received both your letters together—and was so happy (only not about the fact that you are unwell)—and I felt how truly I have come to love you. I felt, not for the first time since I left Petersburg, that you stand for something in my life with which I could never wish to part.

I find myself here in a whirl of events, even more than I did in Petersburg, and I shan't be able to leave before Tuesday. I shall have to return here for the Pushkin centenary celebrations on 25 May. But as you will be leaving Petersburg on 15 May, I am afraid that we might "miss one another" as they say in Little Russia. And since I should hate this to happen, may I ask you to let me know at the following address ... on what day and exactly by which train (there are three trains: at 12.30, at 4 and 8 o'clock) you propose to set off from Moscow along the Kursk route. Once I have this information, I can wait for you at Mtsensk station and travel with you to Oryol. I should dearly like to ask you to stay with me at my place—it's a mere 10 verst from Mtsensk—but this might cause you some inconvenience as you will not be travelling alone and will have lots of luggage and so on. But do not forget to let me know.

At the very moment on the day of my departure when you were standing in church and looking at your watch, I for my part was gazing at the station entrance hoping that, possibly ... It turned out that my request to you not to see me off was sheer stupidity. But you were not justified in attributing this stupidity to the motive you mentioned. I simply did not want to say good-bye to you surrounded by a crowd—as it turned out, there was no crowd. I don't find it easy to forget you—but then, I don't really want to.

I did not send you the snapshot with the little hat, because I seem to remember that you did not like it.

Don't trouble to write me long letters in the middle of all your preoccupations which will soon become a heavy burden. I shall be quite content with a postcard bearing the words, "I am well"—and perhaps you might add, "I extend my hand to you: you may kiss it". I am doing just that now in my thoughts—and not once only; and I hope to do it in reality at Mtsensk. Meanwhile keep well, do not give in to depression, and believe in the sincere attachment of,

your Ivan Turgenev.

P.S. Ostrovsky has just left me—he asked me to convey his greetings to you. He loves you very much and has a high regard for you.[24]

["Little Russia" was the contemporary name for the Ukraine; the verb *razminutsia* which Turgenev uses was at that time largely confined to this region though it is now established as standard usage.]

(the same day)
Dear Marya Gavrilovna,

I bet your first thought on getting this letter will be, "That old man seems to be in a writing humour!" Never mind! I still want to say a few words to you. First, about the card from Mukhortova congratulating you—I don't think she was hinting at anything. She is a good, frank sort of woman. She simply wanted to make up for her forgetfulness on the first day of the holidays. Second, about the new play in which you appeared. It is probably a poor piece of work and it's just too bad that you have to burden your memory with words which you will soon afterwards throw out of your head. But you can claim so many triumphs that this inferior stuff is not really important. Third, I have just returned from the theatre, where I saw "A Tasty Morsel". Ilyinskaya, who played the part of the *ingénue*, is aping you, though she has a spark—no more—of her own. Fedorova is positively insufferable: affected, all airs and graces, disgustingly flirtatious, and so self-assured that I could cheerfully have buried her alive with my own hands. However, young Sadovsky (the son) promises in time to become a great actor. He is natural, passionate, good-natured, and has some of the attractive, quiet humour which his father possessed so abundantly. The play itself is thoroughly bad—bits of French taffeta sewn together with coarse Russian thread.

Well, goodbye then—or rather *au revoir*, as you said on your card. I am already dreaming of our travelling together in the train from Mtsensk to Oryol. How I will kiss your charming hands to my heart's content! Keep well.

Your friend, Ivan Turgenev.

P.S. I met Strepetova at Pisemsky's. She inspires great pity—looks half dead.[25]

[The play which Turgenev disliked so much had been adapted by Krylov from the French comedy, *Nos Alliées*. His high opinion of the younger Sadovsky was borne out in time, when the latter became one of the greatest actors in the Russian theatre. Strepetova was in a state of emotional suffering caused by strained relations with her husband.]

(Moscow, 9 May 1880)

You are spoiling me with your letters—and I am most grateful to you. Owing to the great number of engagements here, I am not leaving Moscow until Wednesday. I shall arrive in the country on Friday, and shall not budge from there but simply wait for your news until I go to meet you at Mtsensk. You set my imagination on fire when you wrote, "It is very possible that I shall send my travelling companions on the Warsaw route while I set out for Moscow." I began to picture a couple of days at my own Spasskoye such as would not easily come again. But should you wish to visit me with your travelling companions, I would find room for them—my house is quite large.

Of course, if you came on your own—"Not a word more, just silence", as Gogol says in *Notes of a Madman*.

I am very glad that you are not complaining of ill health; but your depression—this does not please me, and yet it does . . . puzzle out the why and wherefore of this for yourself. Whose *Don Juan* are you playing? Pushkin's? What part did you take? Laura? or perhaps Donna Anna?

Here I am still dashing about like a cat on hot bricks. Two days ago I made the acquaintance of twenty-two nephews and nieces—all at once! I had not even suspected their existence. I cannot say that the meeting gave me great pleasure.

I think of you often—more often than I ought. You have imprinted yourself deeply on my heart.

As soon as I arrive in the country I will write to you and begin to wait. They have asked me to write something for the Pushkin centenary celebrations but I don't yet know how I'll manage it.

My thanks for "both hands". I take them again and kiss them—very tenderly and very lingeringly. I love you.

Yours, Iv. Turgenev.[26]

(Spasskoye, 17 May 1880)
Dear Marya Gavrilovna,

I arrived here yesterday to find everything in order and in bloom and I am hastening to let you have this information: there are three trains leaving Moscow for Mtsensk and beyond.

(1) the express which leaves Moscow at 12.30 p.m. and arrives at Mtsensk at 10 in the evening (this is the train I took yesterday); (2) the mail train which leaves at 4 p.m. and arrives at 4.30 the following morning; (3) the slow train which leaves at 8.30 in the evening, arriving at 9.45 the following morning.

Do not forget to send me a wire (to Mtsensk) in good time, telling me on what day and by what train you are leaving Moscow. And I shall meet you at Mtsensk and either come with you as far as Oryol or take you to my place—in one or two carriages depending whether you want to stay with me on your own or with your companions. I have plenty of spare rooms and even the cook is turning out all right, so you should all be comfortable. The garden is at its best. You will stay with me at least twenty-four hours—if you can't manage longer—and then I will take you back to Mtsensk (where you will have deposited your luggage) and, with my parting blessing, let you go on to Odessa. Che ne dite, Signorina?

Please let me have your answer at once; it is ages since I have seen your handwriting. I kiss your dear hands and remain for ever,

Yours, Iv. Turgenev.[27]

(two days later)

C'est encore moi. I am writing to you (though I'm not at all sure whether my letter will catch you still in Petersburg) to ask you to let me know when you wire if you are going to visit me on your own. Of course you'll have your personal maid, but what about your travelling companions—that is, unless you have given up the idea of visiting me at all? When I know, I can make the necessary arrangements. I sincerely hope that you will come and that you will not be bored. My garden is delightful just now.

I kiss your hands and remain your old friend Iv. Turgenev.[28]

(Spasskoye, 23 May 1880)

I am pestering you, dear Marya Gavrilovna, but then, what am I to do? I was hoping that you would write from Petersburg when you were leaving and would wire from Moscow, where you will probably stop for at least a day. But you are silent, and that is why I repeat my threefold question: will you visit me in the country—when—and how many people, if any, will accompany you? I have sent you a railway timetable. I still think that the most convenient train for you is the express that leaves Moscow at 12.30 and arrives at Mtsensk at 9.55.

I kiss your lazy little hand and remain yours,
Iv. Turgenev.[29]

[Savina did not stay at Spasskoye on this occasion, but they travelled together from Mtsensk to Oryol on 28 May as Turgenev had planned. Short though the journey was, it brought happiness to Turgenev, and yet ... He wrote to her next day:]

Dear Marya Gavrilovna,

It is half past twelve. I got home an hour and a half ago, and here I am writing to you. I spent the night in Oryol—and a very good night it was because my mind was full of you all the time. Yet not so very good, because I could not close my eyes. I hope that you, in your comfortable compartment, slept better than I did. In my thoughts I came on with you to Kiev. Today is the day I had intended for your stay at Spasskoye and, as if by order, it is a heavenly day. Not a cloud in the sky, windless and warm ... Had you been here, you and I and Raisa Alexeyevna would be sitting on the terrace while I talked about impersonal things. But in my real thoughts I should all the time be kissing your little feet in an ecstasy of gratitude. This, at least, is what I dreamed of ... but dreams have remained just dreams. One ought to drive them away, but it's not easy.

I suppose you'll be kind enough to drop me a line when you arrive.

I haven't had a chance to talk to you about the dark shadow over your future. I think I can guess what it is all about, but I should like to be more certain.

Before leaving the station last night, while you were at the open window of your compartment where I had stood before you in silence, I muttered to myself, "desperate one". You seemed to think that I meant you, but I had in mind something quite different.

A *desperate* thought almost persuaded me to seize you and carry you off the station. The third station bell would have sounded, followed by a desperate cry from Raisa Alexeyevna and perhaps you too, but it would already have been too late. You would have had to stay with me for the next twenty-four hours—but where—and how? Yes, that was the thought that made me say "desperate". But—unfortunately—my good sense prevailed, the station bell sounded, and "ciao" as the Italians say.

But just imagine what the papers would have made of it! I can just see the headline "Scandal at Orlov station" and then —"An extraordinary happening occurred here yesterday. The writer Turgenev (by no means a young man) was seeing off the famous actress Savina who was travelling to Odessa to fulfil a star engagement. Suddenly, as the train was about to draw out of the station, he dragged Mme Savina from the window of her compartment, despite her desperate objections, as if possessed by a demon . . ." and so on and so on. What a sensation to shake the whole of Russia! And yet, it could have happened—it hung by a thread: so, incidentally, does everything in life.

And so—I am here until the twenty-fourth; after that three

days in Petersburg and then to Paris and Bougival at Les Frênes. How long I shall stay there is as yet undecided. I must confess that I have not much faith in your trip abroad—what *might* have been is not likely to be repeated for me—but just in case, here is a reliable address—M. I. Tourguéneff, Paris, au bureau de poste restante de la rue Milton. But do send me a little note first, at rue de Douai, 50, to say when you plan to arrive, and then write to poste restante giving me your address and so on. But on this occasion: si le verrou doit rester fermé, better not to write at all, for you should remember from mythology in what position Tantalus found himself. I must stop.

I wish you all the best, starting with your health. Regards to your pleasant travelling-companion ... while I kiss your little hands, your little feet, kiss everything you will allow me to kiss, and even that which you will not.

Yours Iv. Turgenev.[30]

P.S. I can write con tutta libertà, can't I—I mean, no one but you will read this? For this reason I am sealing this letter with Pushkin's talisman ring.

[Raisa Alexeyevna was an actress-friend of Savina's who travelled with her to Odessa. The unhappiness about the future to which Turgenev refers must have concerned Savina's relations with her husband-to-be, N. N. Vsevolozhsky.

The ring with which Turgenev sealed the letter was of gold, with a cornelian seal; he described it thus: "This ring was given to Pushkin in Odessa by Princess Vorontsova. Pushkin always wore it—he wrote his poem the *Talisman* about it—and on his deathbed he gave it to the poet Zhukovsky, who in turn gave it to me." After Turgenev's death the ring became the property of Pauline Viardot, who presented it to the Pushkin Museum at the Alexander Lycée, from where it was stolen in 1919. It was not in fact a talisman, but a seal inscribed in

Hebrew: "Simkha, son of the venerable rabbi Joseph the elder, may his memory be blessed."]

(31 May 1880)
Dear Marya Gavrilovna,

Really, this is ridiculous. The weather here is heavenly for the third day in succession. I walk in the park from morning to evening or sit on the terrace. I try to think—and I do think—about all kinds of things, yet somewhere deep down there sounds only a single note. I deceive myself that I am thinking about the Pushkin centenary celebrations and suddenly I realize that my lips are whispering, "What a night it could have been . . . but what would have happened later, God only knows!" And at the same time there comes the realization that this will never come true and that I shall one day go into the undiscovered country, not bearing with me the memories of something never experienced by me before. For some reason, it seems to me that we shall never meet again. I did not previously have faith that you will go abroad, and I still have none—and I shall not come to Petersburg in the winter. You have no need to reproach yourself, calling me "your sin"! Alas! I will never be your sin. And, should we meet again in two or three years, then I shall be quite an old man, you will have settled down at last, and nothing of the past will remain. This will not affect you overmuch, for you have all your life before you and mine is behind me—and that hour in the train when I felt almost like a young man of twenty, was the last flicker of the holy lamp. It is difficult even to explain what kind of feelings you have aroused in me. Am I in love with you? I do not know—in the past, such things were different. This irresistible desire to merge, to possess—and to surrender—when even the urging of the flesh loses itself in a kind of lambent flame—I am probably babbling, but I should have been immeasurably happy if only—if only . . .

And now, knowing that this is not to be, I cannot say that I am unhappy or even particularly sad, but I deeply regret that this enchanting night has been lost for ever without brushing me with its wing. I am sorry for my own sake and, dare I add, for yours too—for I am sure you would not have forgotten the happiness you gave me.

I should not have written so much had I not felt that this is a letter of farewell. I do not mean to suggest that our correspondence will stop—no, no, I hope that we shall often exchange news—but the door which was partly opened and behind which some unrevealed wonder was beckoning, has been slammed for ever. One can truly say, le verrou est tiré. Whatever may happen, I shall no longer be the same—nor will you.

Well, that will do. What has been—or not been!—has blossomed and withered. But that does not prevent me from wishing you the very best in the world, and in my thoughts I kiss your dear hands. You do not have to reply to this letter—but do answer the first one.

Yours, Iv. Turgenev.

P.S. You need have no fear for the future. Such a letter you will never receive again.[31]

[This is the sad, intimate letter which Savina did not trust herself to keep, gave to Koni, but later retrieved and burned; see p. 8. The next letter, referring to it, was written to her by Koni two years after Turgenev's death.]

(Kissingen, Villa Csillagom, 29 July 1885)

Today, my dear Marya Gavrilovna, I received a pile of letters sent to me on 1 July and addressed to me at Petersburg during my absence; among them was yours, so precious and sparkling with intelligence, wit and talent. I am answering at once lest my reply should miss you at Siva.

I will begin with the question of Turgenev's letter. What reasons prompted you to give me this letter? Clearly, one neither tears up this kind of thing nor throws it away, however earnestly he may have begged you to do so. You have carried out his wish: the letter is no longer in your possession, but in hands that opened it with awe and have hidden it away in the holy of holies. It is indeed like an unpublished prose-poem. If you were not Savina, this letter would in years to come proudly declare who you were in your private life—you could show it to your grandchildren and say to them, "Look!"

Thank God, you have no need of this. The sun called Turgenev need not lend its rays to the light of the planet called Savina—a light that sheds such grace, intelligence and talent. But that makes this letter all the more precious. What "daring purity" of thought, what language, what true poetry, are in this letter! He is all there—this Mont Blanc of Russian literature with his pure heart so easily set aflame by all things beautiful. But you, Marya Gavrilovna, you emerge from this letter like an antique statue straight from the sculptor's hands. Seen through the eyes of Turgenev, you dazzle every reader, you convey a sense of harmony, wholeness and fascination— and at the same time of detachment and withdrawal—as withdrawn as the goddess of Milo who boldly reveals to mortal eyes the charms of her divine form. And I am pleased by this withdrawal. Anything else would have been commonplace and unworthy of you and Turgenev. You stayed with him like the Ellis of his *Phantoms* and remained Ellis-like in his memory, incorporeal and fascinating. This letter should give you every right to feel proud, to realize your superiority to the multitude. I am deeply grateful to you for having given it to me. I do not know how to be worthy of such trust. But should you one day change your mind, just say the word and the letter will be placed intact at your feet, where once before it was laid.[32]

[As Turgenev had prophesied, the correspondence continued in a different key, though emotion still broke through from time to time. A week after the "farewell" letter, Turgenev sent a telegram to Savina who was appearing at Odessa—his excuse was the possibility of a closure of the theatres following the death of the Empress Marya Alexandrovna—"Should the theatre be temporarily closed, won't you break your journey at Spasskoye? I shall be staying there from 29 May to 3 June. If this is all right wire me in Moscow. Fix a day of arrival at Mtsensk. Turgenev." Meanwhile, he had a letter from Savina and wrote in reply:]

(Moscow, 8 June 1880)
Dear Marya Gavrilovna,

To drown yourself in the sea? Are you not ashamed to write this? Of course the idea came to you in a moment of depression—but all the same! And those charming hands which were such a joy to kiss—would you really have given them to the fishes to eat? Allow me to tweak your little ear gently. And in future, don't upset your friends.

I have received both your letters and your telegram. It seems that you will continue your performances (I hope that the Odessa critics will show more sense than those whose samples of intelligence you sent me) and that you will stay there until 1 July... And then? God only knows! Our Pushkin celebrations have been put off until Wednesday, 17 June; on the 18th and 19th I shall still be in Moscow, and then I shall set off via Petersburg for Bougival, where I hope to arrive on the 22nd. I thought I had developed rather a bad attack of rheumatism but today, thanks to the energetic measures of the doctor... I am continuing the letter—Wednesday, 9 June: I am not a bit better and shall most likely stick in Moscow right up to 17 June.

I am waiting for the promised letter. I hope that you are no longer depressed and, as the pedants say, are devoting yourself *wholeheartedly to art*. I do not know when and where we shall meet—but I do know that I shall be happy to see you. My regards to your agreeable travelling companion—and I remain, with love,

yours Iv. Turgenev.[33]

[Savina was not enjoying her engagement in Odessa, and the suicide threat seems to have featured widely in her correspondence at the time. She wrote to Toporov: "At present my existence here is merely waiting for 1 July, that is, the day of my departure. Should something prevent it, I'll drown myself. The company is impossible, the theatre is more like a fairground." On the eve of the Pushkin celebrations, Turgenev wrote to her again:]

(Moscow, 16 June 1880)
Dear Marya Gavrilovna,

I sent you a wire this morning in answer to your kind enquiry and now I am writing to you. I have been really unwell; on arriving in Moscow I did not leave the house for five days because of a sharp attack of rheumatism in the shoulder, but I have improved now and am deeply involved in preparations for the celebration, which begins tomorrow. There is frightful turmoil here, but it looks as if things will go off all right; and on Monday night I am returning to Spasskoye by the very same train—you remember?—which you took. The following Thursday I am leaving straight for Paris, that is, for Bougival. Although for some reason I cannot really believe in your trip abroad—however, if you do come to Paris give me fair warning and let me know—and not by poste restante but direct to Bougival. I am very curious to know what you have written in the registered letter sent to my Spasskoye address. So far I have not received it. Avez-vous fermé—ou bien ouvert —le verrou? However I twist and turn, you have me in your net—and I spoke the truth when I said that you have brought into my life something from which I shall never part.

I hope that life is pleasant in Odessa and that theatre affairs run their prescribed course—and that your charming eyes are no longer dimmed by depression. If I remember rightly, you told me that you would stay in Odessa until 1 July—and then straight to Petersburg? If you write to me in Petersburg as soon as you receive this, your letter might just catch me. When are you starting your run in Petersburg?

Give my regards to your travelling companion: I have met her father here. And you... what am I to do with you? Yes, I would know what... but for the moment I am content to take your hands and kiss them slowly and tenderly, while you are looking on and thinking—what? But that's enough; keep yourself well, and, perhaps, au revoir.

Yours, Iv. Turgenev.

P.S. Have you seen that your papers have trumpeted about my visiting Odessa? It might have happened—but it did not.[34]

(Spasskoye, 23 June 1880)
Dear Marya Gavrilovna,

I arrived here only this morning and am not too well; I have suffered a sharp attack of rheumatism in my right shoulder. In addition, I am terribly tired from those celebrations, magnificent though they were. I shall stay here five days altogether and then go straight to France. I have received your registered letter: thank you for the promise of a meeting. I am sending you my speech as you asked. I do not know how interesting you will find it (it did not seem to make a great impression on the public). This is my only copy, and I ask you not to give it to *anyone either to read or to copy*—as the speech has been promised to the *European Herald*, where it should appear on 1 July. For this reason, I was obliged to refuse all journalists' questions about the speech. You are very wrong to bathe so much—have you not caught cold? I'm completely ignorant about your theatre affairs. I hope—to the credit of all in Odessa—they proceed brilliantly. When does your season come to an end?

Should you wish to reply to this letter straight away—do write to Petersburg, to the office of the *European Herald*. If, on the other hand, you wish to take your time over writing—then to Paris, 50 rue de Douai.

And so, in fact, quite seriously—is it au revoir? In my thoughts I am looking forward to kissing your charming hands—and in Paris? Well, we shall see about all this.

Yours, with love, Iv. Turgenev.[35]

[The speech in question was of course the one which Turgenev had made at the Pushkin celebrations when the Pushkin memorial was unveiled. The rheumatism of which he complained was probably the beginning of his fatal cancer. However, he was well enough to go to France as planned. Savina went too, but with her future husband, to the vexation of Turgenev who opened his heart to Toporov on the subject:]

(Bougival, 29 July 1880)

Savina has been here for a week already, with M. Vsevolozhsky, but she did not think fit to let me know. She evidently has no desire to see me—which does not worry me in the least....[36]

(Bougival, 7 August 1880)

As to Savina, of course I shall not see her—for she must have left without letting me know of her stay in Paris. However, I was not counting at all on seeing her and am only surprised at what she has told you. She has probably done it from an incurable tendency to make up stories which is characteristic of (1) all Russians and (2) all women. However, it is all the same to me...[37]

(Bougival, 21 August 1880)

M. G. Savina is now most likely already in Petersburg. You may see her—but I ask you *not* to give her my regards. It is quite clear that she had no wish to see me, but common courtesy should have made her write just a line. I wish her all possible success, but she has ceased to exist for me.[38]

[Savina did get in touch with Turgenev after all and they met, but not on the old terms.]

(Bougival, 31 August 1880)
Dear Marya Gavrilovna,

I am not very happy about our meeting. We met and parted like polite strangers. I shall be in Paris on Thursday and shall call on you in the morning about 12. If you are at home, we shall have a peaceful chat—about your future roles and so on. I should have been happy to invite you here, or go to the woods of St Germain, or at least to the Bois de Boulogne—but this hardly seems possible. Should I not find you at home, I shall take it that you prefer to say your goodbyes from a distance. In that case, I send you the very best parting wishes.

I could not think of any device for you. Unless like this—the drawing of a theatrical mask or some other symbol of the drama, encircled by the words, "Until the very end"—or, in French, "Jusqu'au bout".

I kiss your hands—I noticed again today how beautiful and interesting they are—and remain,

Your devoted Iv. Turgenev.[39]

(Bougival, 1 September: Telegram)

Impossible de venir demain, jeudi. Voulez-vous vendredi? Un mot de réponse Bougival, Les Frênes, Tourguéneff.[40]

(Paris, 13 November 1880)
Dear Marya Gavrilovna,

I understood very well by the way you shook hands with me on parting at our last meeting in Paris that there was a clear separation between us—though not any hostility—I cannot stop taking an active interest in your destiny and your talent.

You promised to write, but of course you did not believe the words even while you were saying them. Since your return to Petersburg you have acted in some new parts. Won't you let me have some news about them, and about your health, and whether you are soon going to marry? All this is of great interest to me. As for myself, I can say that my health is not too bad. Recently, I have even started writing—something small. I shall probably go to Petersburg towards the end of this year, but whether we shall meet—except at the theatre—is problematic. In any case, when we do meet we shall not be the same: we shall meet—if we do—as different people.

The papers say that you intend to act in Warsaw—in Polish. If I remember rightly, you did mention something of the kind. I clasp your hand warmly and remain,
  your sincerely devoted Iv. Turgenev.[41]

(Paris, 4 December 1880—to Toporov)
Have you passed on my letter to Savina? She has not replied ... she probably wishes to break off all relations with me. Well, if that's what she wishes, let's forget her....[42]

[But it was in a very different mood that Turgenev responded to a letter from Savina three days later:]

(Paris, 7 December 1880)
Dear Marya Gavrilovna,
I received your letter today and, as you see, I am answering it the same day. It gave me great joy—not, indeed, its rather sad contents, but just by arriving. You remember—don't you?—how I once told you that you have set a mark on my life which cannot be effaced, even were I myself to attempt it. That was the truth. But, may I ask, how is it that in drawing up a new contract you could not safeguard your interests and ensure that you were not exploited in such an unheard-of manner? In your position, to act twice a day—and in two

different theatres at that—is monstrous! Or are you, perhaps, in need of such feverish activity in order to suppress—what exactly? One can truly apply to you the saying that is popular here: "Il n'y a que le provisoire qui soit éternel". One lives from day to day, always thinking, "This is only for the moment, for the time being", and suddenly realizing that the whole of life has been lived in that way.

I read in the papers a review of your latest role and was very pleased. You must be excellent in it if even Suvorin praises you. They write that you are charming in the Russian costume—won't you send me a photograph? However, as the poem by Bogdanovich says, "You are lovely, dearest, whatever you may wear". The very same papers report that you have found a play for your benefit performance and that it is one by Potekhin.

Perhaps it will have an interesting role for you, and be worthy of your talent.

You ask me when I shall go to Petersburg. God knows! It depends on various circumstances and events, which may happen soon or may be delayed. In any case, I hope to arrive in Russia not later than January. Of course I will see you, but—the presence of your future husband, which was somewhat of an embarrassment to me in Paris, will make itself felt. The past in its former image cannot be recovered.

As to myself—I have to admit that, though my health is reasonable, I am getting old and am ageing: the two don't always coincide. But what's to be done about it? As the proverb says, one has lived, one has drunk the wine, and now one must retire with dignity.

You have not given me your new address, so I again have to write to you through Toporov. Don't forget to let me have it in your next letter. I wish you all the very best from my innermost heart and kiss your intelligent hands.

Your devoted Ivan Turgenev.[43]

[Once again Savina was not quick to reply and on 25 January 1881, Turgenev ended a letter to Toporov—"Should you see Savina, give her my regards". However, further encouraging news prompted him to write again:]

(Paris, 5 February 1881)
Dear Marya Gavrilovna,

I received a letter from Toporov yesterday; according to him, you intended to send me a telegram with New Year greetings. Unfortunately I did not get it. I say "unfortunately" because this telegram would have proved that you had not forgotten me. And Toporov also told me that the day after tomorrow—7 February—is your name day. My letter won't reach you in time for it, but never mind. I am taking the opportunity of this letter to wish you all possible blessings, beginning with your health, the improvement of your position—and finishing by wishing you plenty of success. I mention this last because there is no need to be anxious about it if everything else is all right—your success is inseparable from you.

I have been rather ill and am even now not quite well. This has interfered with my going to Petersburg and now my trip has been put off to the end of March. But I still hope to find you in Petersburg and even to see you in one of your new parts.

I remember asking you to send me your photograph in that peasant costume in which even Suvorin thought you delightful, but apparently you have other things to occupy your mind. However, if my letter finds you in a generous mood, give a thought to my request.

That faithful Toporov gave me your address, so I am sending my letter to Ivanov Street.

I kiss your hands and remain yours,
Ivan Turgenev.[44]

[Again the waiting, the brief mention of his disappointment—"I have not had a reply from Polonsky. Nor from M. G. Savina", he wrote to Toporov on 19 February. Then a letter which, as before, he answered immediately:]

(Paris, 13 March 1881)
Dear Marya Gavrilovna,

This morning I received your letter. To begin with I was glad—just because it had come, because of its length and a few kind words—for which I at once ask leave to kiss all the little fingers of your right hand. But then your letter saddened me by its contents and the bad news about your health. If you persist in not sparing yourself, you are bound to wear yourself out. And, quite seriously, I invite you to give me the honour and pleasure of coming and resting for a few days—or weeks—at my place in the country this summer.

You may have heard already that the youngest daughter of Mme Viardot, my dear Marianne, is going to be married; the wedding has been fixed for between 3 and 10 April. I shall be leaving two days later for Petersburg, where I hope to arrive about 15 April, and on St Nicholas' Day, 21 May, I should be at home at Spasskoye, where I shall remain all through the summer. Assuming that your vacation will be starting from May, I believe nothing better could be planned for your health than a carefree, quiet stay in the country. At my Spasskoye the climate is fine, the garden beautiful, the house newly-decorated, and the cook excellent. I shall spoil you—a delightful thought. And as the Polonskys will be staying, propriety will be observed. And so, perhaps, last year's dream will come true. Think it over and write to me, so that I can be happy in advance.

I have read in the papers about your triumphs and the ovations you have received, and have been truly glad. When all is said, a link that nothing can break has been forged between you and me. Incidentally, the author of your benefit play—is it the same Tchaikovsky about whom you once talked to me—do you remember?

And one more question! I see that your divorce proceedings are going forward. What is the reason? Is it to marry M. Vsevolozhsky? Do, please, give me an answer to this as well. Or perhaps you simply want to be free?

And you have not sent me the photograph after all . . . If I had it, I should bow low enough to kiss your little feet.

I can imagine how Dostoyevsky's funeral must have affected you—and then the funeral of Levkeyeva. With a nervous system like yours, great care is needed—and why was there no good friend at hand to restrain you from driving yourself to exhaustion?

As to myself—I haven't spent a very gay winter. The gout, that had not bothered me for the past three years, has badly tormented me and I still walk as if on pitchforks. I am getting old—what's to be done about it?—and only certain memories have power to kindle the old fire in me.

[Turgenev heard the news of the assassination of the Emperor Alexander II on this day and continued his letter two days later.]

I had interrupted the letter, intending to continue, and suddenly this terrible news arrived. I won't go into the details of it, but will only say that now, when theatres will most probably be closed for about three months, my invitation to you seems very opportune. Do come to stay with me at Spasskoye at the beginning of May—for, well, at least two weeks—and from there you can if necessary set off for the Crimea, for a spa, for Paris—wherever you may want to go. This would be so good, and your health would improve on our black-earth land! And how beautifully we should pass the time! Do not wait for my arrival in Petersburg to let me have your decision.

In any case, it is scarcely a month before I shall see you. You say at the end of your letters, "I kiss you affectionately". What does it mean? As it was then, on that June night, in the train? Should I live for a hundred years, I will not forget those kisses. I dare to believe that this was in your mind.

Dear Marya Gavrilovna, I love you very much—much more than I ought to, but it is not my fault. I hope your health has improved, and I ask you not to forget your Ivan Turgenev.[45]

(Paris, 6 April 1881)
Dear Marya Gavrilovna,

Yesterday my darling Marianne was married to the talented young composer Duvernua. They went off together on the same day. Their marriage will probably be a very happy one—they truly love one another and are admirably suited in character. Needless to say, I am pleased, even happy, although of course the house is empty. But to make up for it, there is the knowledge that *she* is happy—and this is the main thing.

In a week I am leaving for Petersburg and in about ten days we shall meet, which will be a great joy for me.

Three days before the wedding I received your dear letter (although without your picture in the Russian costume) and as I do not know of hands that are more gratifying to kiss than yours, I am kissing them—just in my imagination for the time being.

Thank you for your promise to visit me at Spasskoye. Let us see how you will keep that promise. I hope that you will not be too bored under my roof—but in any case your health should improve.

I can well imagine how your nerves must have been affected by all these terrible events—and then the enforced inactivity. You will be doing nothing when you are with me in the country too—but it will be different.

I will let you know the date of my arrival. How pleasant, how delightful, it will be to see your beautiful eyes again!

Especially if I should detect at least a spark of pleasure in them. Au revoir! I kiss your hands again and remain your truly loving Ivan Turgenev.[46]

[Turgenev was right in thinking that the funeral of Dostoyevsky, coming as it did close upon that of the actress Levkeyeva, would increase Savina's depression. This is how Koni described the scene:]

Dostoyevsky's funeral deeply affected Savina. They had so often taken part in public readings together. Along with other representatives of the Russian stage, she took part in the funeral, which was a public event without precedent.

There was a complete absence of police "precautions", but the unending huge march was entirely orderly. Order was maintained by a line of students. There was impressive singing by countless impromptu choirs. Pupils from high schools lined the route of the procession; there were innumerable wreaths with affecting inscriptions, carried by special deputations. The mood of both participants and onlookers was solemn and sincere. All this gave the procession a majestic appearance and a quality never to be forgotten. Everyone felt united in the common realization of loss—a unifying force that established a bond between people totally different in outlook, position and interests.

All this could not fail to affect the impressionable Savina; she suffered nervous and bodily strain from that heightened mood and physical exhaustion.[47]

[Before the long-awaited visit to Spasskoye took place Turgenev and Savina met in Moscow.]

(Moscow, 26 June 1881)
Dear Marya Gavrilovna,

I am leaving today so I shall not have the great joy of seeing you. When I get to Spasskoye I will immediately prepare a room for you and will wait for you to let me know when I can meet you at Mtsensk. Perhaps you will write in advance from Petersburg.

Yesterday restored much to me. I kiss your little hands and remain your Ivan Turgenev, affectionate and expecting you.

P.S. Bring your stage-parts; I hope we shall make good use of our time together.

P.P.S. My country address is Orlovskaya District, Mtsensk, the village of Spasskoye-Lutovinovo.[48]

[The day in Moscow remained in Savina's memory too, and she described it in a letter to Bazilevsky from Warsaw, 24 February 1895:]

For all its dreadful faults, I love Moscow very much—but just as you do, as a tourist. Unfortunately I cannot put on the cap of Fortunatus, so my stay there gets spoilt. The Church of Our Redeemer is truly a wonder! Ivan Sergeyevich and I went over it while it was being built. He thought that the interior was too light and it seemed that the sacred pictures—notably the one of St Mary Magdalene—did not answer their purpose. He said, "Art and splendour are too distracting here, and it is difficult to pray in this church." He preferred St Isaac's Cathedral because of the severity of its style. I find the Church of Our Redeemer most comforting, and the iconostasis has staggered me in the fullest sense of the word. Happy are those who have unquestioning faith![49]

[In 1881 Savina was already doing the kind of charitable work which she developed in later years—notably her foundation of a home for aged actors. Turgenev supported an unidentified project, referred to in a letter written just after the farewell note of 26 June:]

An hour ago I sent you a note, and now I want to say that I have informed Maslov through Fedor (my valet) about your intention. Maslov is in Ilyinskoye and I shall not have a chance of seeing him. However, you will see him and talk things over with him. He will gladly help you in your noble undertaking. Incidentally, I shall leave ten roubles to be given to him, which he will add to your subscription.

And so, au revoir at Spasskoye—and in the meantime, keep well and cheerful.

Your sincerely loving Ivan Turgenev.[50]

[At last Savina came to Spasskoye. The story of her visit was told by Polonsky, who was also staying there with his family. As will appear later, Savina disagreed with some of Polonsky's impressions; but let him speak first, for we shall rarely see Turgenev so completely happy again:]

Count Tolstoy had just left when Marya Gavrilovna Savina arrived at Spasskoye. Ivan Sergeyevich had long given up expecting her; he even had a bet with me that she would not come. With her arrival the weather changed for the better, but on 16 July when we were dining on the terrace a sudden hailstorm swooped down. In an instant the dining table was spattered with hail and when we hurried indoors the glass in the door broke into splinters. Our dinner was, with difficulty, carried into the dining room. Next day my wife and I celebrated our wedding anniversary. At dinner Ivan Sergeyevich made a speech, kept on pouring out champagne, clinking glasses all round and kissing everyone.

On the lake where a kind of bathing-hut stood, Ivan Sergeyevich had a raised wooden platform built. The water near the bathing-hut was very shallow and Savina loved to fling herself into the deep water—she swam like a naiad. On the day of our wedding anniversary (but chiefly in honour of his dear visitor) Ivan Sergeyevich called together the village women and set in motion festivities, with wine and presents, like those which he had been given when he arrived at

Spasskoye. There were a great many women and young girls from the village; singing and dancing once again.

Apparently our actress was watching them with an observant eye, taking note of their tunes and movements, and towards the end she had become so gay that she too was almost dancing. "What do you think of that?" Turgenev said to me. "Do you see the gypsy blood rising?"

He himself was so gay that he was ready to give himself up completely to the dancing. At no other time, of course, would he have tolerated my bad piano-playing—but now he urged me to play dance-tunes. Alas! The folk songs I could manage somehow and I could also get away with the polka, but the mazurka did not come easily. "Go on playing!" Turgenev shouted to me—"as you like, as you can, but go on! Go on with the mazurka! As long as there is music—One, two, three—stress the *one*—Come on! Come on!" And all through the evening until tea was served all were dancing as well as they could.

I do not remember whether it was the same night or another when, in his study late in the evening, Turgenev for the first time read to Savina and to us his story *The Song of Triumphant Love*. The ladies were much impressed by it and I admired it greatly. The following day, Marya Gavrilovna with her personal maid stepped into the carriage and left Spasskoye for good.[51]

[According to Savina, however, Polonsky was not very appreciative of the reading, and was inaccurate in other ways. We need not expect complete agreement in the accounts of those who saw Turgenev from very different angles. What matters now is the memory that Savina retained after Turgenev was dead. Her own impression of that visit can be pieced together from various sources: a letter to Belyayev in 1903, a conversation recorded by D. Filosofov, a letter to Bazilevsky in 1895. All the words that follow are her own, woven into a continuous account in which nostalgia is mingled with happiness: "I felt unbearably saddened by the memories that came rushing to my mind", she wrote to Belyayev when she read his description of those days:]

The fact that the "Petersburg Undine" swam in the lake at Spasskoye has been immortalized by the absurd reminiscences of Polonsky, but far more interesting is the fact that Turgenev himself, with the help of Polonsky, knocked together a kind of bathing-hut from odd boards because Zhosefina Antonovna —Polonsky's wife—and I felt too embarrassed to bathe otherwise. And Ivan Sergeyevich himself drove me and the Polonsky children to the lake in a racing gig. He looked amazingly handsome, in a big straw hat, a Parisian brown knitted jacket with silk sleeves and a loosely-tied white kerchief instead of a tie. He drove the horse with great pleasure, like a child, and the smile never left his face. In the woods he gathered flowers more eagerly than the rest of us and chatted away incessantly.

When I entered his study for the first time, Ivan Sergeyevich said, quite simply, "Here at this table I wrote *Fathers and Sons*."

He had a strong attachment to the screens by his bedside. His mother had brought home from Sorrento an album with a cover made from wooden mosaic and, showing it to her serf-joiner, ordered him to make screens after that mosaic model. "Semyon" or "Yakov", having not the slightest idea of inlaid woodwork, took for his model fruits in their natural colours and so made those delightful screens.

On the table there always stood a vase with some of the roses that grew in front of the balcony. From the garden, there drifted the scent of limes in the avenue which Ivan Sergeyevich himself had planted. A laden branch reached through the open window by the desk. A large ikon of the Saviour, which had belonged to his mother Varvara Petrovna, looked severely from a corner. Ivan Sergeyevich would sit in the big leather armchair—this, too, had belonged to his mother—while I sat at his feet on a leather stool and listened to the *Poems in Prose*. Yes, I was a lucky girl. Ivan Sergeyevich would take out of the desk-drawer a large book bound in green leather and would read and read, while the tears streamed down my cheeks. He had read to me this story of the great, overmastering love for a woman to whom a whole life had been given and who would not bring one little flower or shed a single tear on the writer's grave. When I asked him why it should not be published, he replied: "It might hurt her."

On the eve of my departure, we were all sitting on the balcony when Turgenev said, "I want to read you something I have written." Very agitatedly, he went to his study to fetch the manuscript of *The Song of Triumphant Love*. He asked whether we liked it. What could I answer? I had not fully understood it and did not know how to make an intelligent response. Yet I certainly liked it very much.

Polonsky said straight out, "It's no good. I advise you not to have it published. They won't understand it and they will abuse you." Ivan Sergeyevich was upset. I wanted to comfort him, but my woman's instinct told me that I could not do it with words or reasoned argument. And I had nothing clever to say.

It was about two in the morning. Ivan Sergeyevich said, "Come and listen to the voices of the night." Of course, I was ready to go, though I did not know what he meant and was frightened of the dark, and the unfamiliar surroundings. He led me by the hand about the places he knew so well, while he explained each individual sound to me, sensing rather than actually hearing. My God, what wonderful music is in the "Voices of the night". It seemed as if every blade of grass, every bush, was singing. We walked for a long time, until dawn. When the birds began to waken he called each one by its name; he could foretell which of them would waken first and how it would sing. It was good then. And how he thanked me!

In the end it has turned out that I, silly girl that I was, had more judgement than Polonsky. *The Song of Triumphant Love* is a remarkable piece after all. I could now explain to him why I liked it so much then.[52]

[Belyayev wrote an account of the Spasskoye visit, based on what Savina told him. The friendly way in which she wrote to him about it, quoted previously, suggests that she was satisfied with its accuracy. Belyayev gives some interesting information to supplement her own account:]

Turgenev presented Savina with a blue book. "Here you are," he said, "if you care to, do some writing." "But what shall I write?" said Savina with a laugh. "Write what you have told me, in the way that you told it."

What was it that Savina told Turgenev? She told him about her life in the theatre, about her hopes; and the old writer listened like a good-natured grandpa to this lively, witty talk, interrupting her from time to time with, "Excellent . . . that's it . . . you talk well." And after one of these talks he would add, "You must write this down, you are sure to have a good style." "I can't," Savina would start to make excuses—"I can't keep a diary, and as soon as I sit down at a table and start writing, I so much want to be clever that I get disgusted at making literature."

Turgenev smiled: "Making literature—that's good."

It was summer when Savina stayed at Spasskoye. After a hot day, when the cool evening descended, Turgenev would come out of his room on to the balcony and say to his visitor, "Well, now, what about making your confession?"

They called these talks "confessions"; and indeed Savina

seemed inspired and sometimes the confession lasted late into the night. Turgenev would listen to her, his eyes half closed, still smiling. The new moon would rise into the sky above the garden, a mist would drift from the lake ... and indoors the hissing samovar would have been long awaiting them.[53]

[Polonsky and his wife remained at Spasskoye for a time after Savina had gone. Turgenev writes at first with the new vigour and enthusiasm which Savina's visit had aroused in him, but his happiness is shadowed by her impending marriage to Nikita Nikitich Vsevolozhsky. She had gone to the latter's estate at Siva, in the Perm province.]

(Spasskoye, 3 August 1881)
Dear Marya Gavrilovna,

I have just returned from a two-day business trip to the Yefremov district, and have found your letter and telegram here. Needless to say, the news you sent has gladdened me. Setting aside all pride, I was delighted to realize that my forecast was wrong—and I might have lost another wager on your terms. By the way, this convinced me that the *other party* turned out to be less overwrought than I feared. But I shall not feel entirely reassured on your behalf until I hear from you of your journey to Perm—or from Perm itself. I have news of you only up to Monday night—yet you had to stay in Moscow for another twenty-four hours—time for a new "move" to take place, thinking in terms of a game of chess. Let us hope that everything passed off safely and will continue to do so. May you still fall asleep with that calm conscience and that quiet sense of dissatisfaction, even of sadness, which through the will of fate always goes with accomplished duty. Only try not to become bored, for this is where the chief danger lies.

Your stay at Spasskoye left unforgettable impressions. We

all keep talking of you and remembering you. We are all fond of you, and you know that I am truly and sincerely attached to you; I trust that you have proof enough of this not to doubt it. In those five days I came to know you better than ever—with all your strong and weak points—and just because of this attachment became even stronger. You have a friend in me whom you can trust.

The room where you stayed will for ever remain "The Savina Room".

After your departure our life resumed its old routine. Marfa shows her hair under her kerchief more than ever, and the look in her eyes seems to have become more questioning and more thoughtful. Yesterday, however, she was washing floors—an inartistic occupation and position with which, as far as I remember, not a single sentimental novel begins. Can you imagine such a scene in the theatre, with the young heroine finding herself in such a position? Would you take on a role like that? You do indeed, like the true artist you are, seek out difficulties—after all, you have chosen the part of Glafira. [A character in *The Forgotten Country Seat* by Shpazhinsky.] But *this* you would not take upon yourself! Your charming clean hands in dirty water! By the way, I imagine that Glafira must quite certainly have had dirty fingernails—but there is no need for this amount of realism in the accurate portrayal of a character. On the other hand, I think I should have kissed even your grubby little hands with pleasure; but then my attitude to you puts me in an unusual position.

I am counting on your promise to write to me, and I can guarantee prompt answers. You are very attractive and very intelligent—the two don't always go together—and it is delightful to talk to you both in writing and face to face.

They write that Ilyinskaya had a great success in Petersburg. As far as my memory of her goes, she is in no way a rival to you. Has your contract been signed yet? Write and tell me what is your impression of the new play by Shpazhinsky. If I were a dramatist, what a good part I should have thought up for you!

Goodbye for now. Keep well and cheerful. All here send their regards and I, if you will permit me, kiss you with the tenderness of—if not a father, then of an uncle.

Yours, with true devotion, Ivan Turgenev.[54]

[Turgenev's promise to bestow Savina's name on the guest-room at Spasskoye was kept, according to the description given by M. A. Shchepkin, son of the famous actor:]

Small doors led from the "casino" and from the study into a little corridor, which in turn led to the "Savina Room". This room was so named in 1881, when Turgenev was staying at his estate for the last time; it was then occupied by M. G. Savina, the famous actress of the Imperial theatres in St Petersburg. This room had always been kept for guests: G. V. Grigorovich stayed there, and L. N. Tolstoy, and in 1872 William Rolston, the well-known English translator of Turgenev, who was visiting Ivan Sergeyevich. For him, Turgenev specially planned festivities with a national character. At the time of Savina's visit to Turgenev, the celebrated poet Yakov Petrovich Polonsky and his family were staying at Spasskoye, where they spent the whole summer.[55]

(Spasskoye, 22 August 1881)
Dear Marya Gavrilovna,

I have just received your letter of 10 August and am sending my reply to your present address, although I cannot tell from your letter whether you have received my first letter addressed to you in Perm. I am most grateful that, in spite of your fatigue and—as you call it—"Chaos of impressions", you have managed to let me have news of your day-to-day life. Your news greatly interested me, since it concerns your future in which I, being deeply attached to you, am closely involved. I was not too surprised by this news, which had seemed almost inevitable from the moment when you decided to go to Perm. Although the situation has its drawbacks, you have all the same taken the most sensible and logical decision. If this should be confirmed by telegram, we will all joyfully drink your health. For myself, I shall wish you happiness with all my heart—without any *chagrin* though with some *apprehension*—once again, on account of that friendship which has made me so attached to you. And if that *other affair* could in fact dissolve so quickly into thin air, and if you are firmly assured that your marriage will in no way interfere with your theatrical career—then why should those who cherish you and love you not rejoice? Besides, after all your commitment, any turning back or even postponing would be unthinkable. Therefore, be sure and send that telegram, but hurry because I shall be leaving Spasskoye in a week. (Polonsky left today, with his son.) For this reason I cannot, though with deep regret, accept your kind "au revoir" in Moscow, since on the day of your departure for Moscow I shall already be at Bougival. I shall not see you before next year, when everything that is happening today will be a thing of yesterday, and at all events your position will be established . . . or clarified. But I am confident that I shall meet you with my former feelings, and I hope that I shall find yours unchanged. How wonderful it would be of you to send a wire to Paris, Rue de Douai 50—or a letter? I shall be waiting for it.

Since you left, our life here has grown very dull. Besides, we are not being spoiled by the weather: God alone knows what nasty things are happening beneath the heavens! After a poor summer, a poor autumn—and perhaps an early winter; this is really too much! I feel strongly drawn to Bougival.

I should have liked to look at you at the moment when the

toast to the bride was proposed. Firstly because it is always pleasant to see your face, and secondly because it ought to have been particularly fascinating just then.

When we meet, (if we meet) you will tell me all about it in that shrewd, artistic but yet frank manner which is so characteristic of you, and with that sweet trust which I deserve—not as the teacher (with a small or a capital letter), but as your best friend.

All your friends here send you many regards, and for my part I plant kisses on those hands which I cannot forget. What happened on the night before you left—do you remember, at dinner on the terrace, after the champagne?—is still harder to forget, but I scarcely dare remind you of it.

Keep well, gay, cheerful and do not forget Ivan Turgenev.[56]

(Spasskoye, 31 August 1881)
My dear Marya Gavrilovna,

You have told me such horrors about your mail service that I have but little hope of my reply to your delightful letter reaching you in time. Today is the 31st of August, but you are leaving on the 11th September and your mail takes twelve days! Also, to my great sorrow, your request cannot be fulfilled. You are leaving Siva (where is this *Siva?*) on the 11th September, and on that very day I am leaving for Bougival, for I shall leave Spasskoye tomorrow and shall stay in Moscow for only twenty-four hours. From this sad fact, there follows a question which is equally sad for me: when and where shall I see you? And by then, will you be Madame Vsevolozhskaya? From your first letter it could be assumed so, but your second letter makes clear only one thing—that *this year's* flirtation has dissolved into thin air. I am very glad that it happened *this year*. We were all pleased to learn that you are well, cheerful and not feeling bored with life. One thing only is unsatisfactory: the role that you have been given is bad. But you will either find another part or change it so that the author will not recognize it.

Spasskoye is still filled with memories of you. Zhosefina Antonovna sends you her regards. When one of our neighbours, a friend of hers, learned that you had stayed here and that she had missed the opportunity of seeing you, she almost choked with disappointment.

As for myself, I am still here in body but already *there* in my thoughts, and I am already beginning to feel the French skin growing beneath the Russian one which I am casting off. In spring I suppose the reverse process will happen. But what will remain unchanged is my sincere and deep feeling of friendship for you—and you have given me great joy by acknowledging that it is sincere and serious. I do hope that you will not leave me without news of yourself—you know my address: Paris, Rue de Douai 50—and I will reply at once.

Just now I am kissing your dear hands and remain, Yours, Ivan Turgenev.[57]

(Bougival, 5 October 1881)

Well then, my dear Marya Gavrilovna, why this silence? Or are you cross with me for not waiting for you in Moscow? Or is it really just, *enough*? Only think, you left me in complete ignorance about your fate and not even knowing by what name to address you. I wrote to Toporov to find out about you, but he had not had the honour of any notice from you. For some reason or other they do not mention you in the papers. And so I have decided to turn directly to you, remembering the saying "Il vaut mieux s'adresser à Dieu qu'à ses saints". Well then, my dear divinity, will you grant me a few words, and what will they be? I shall await them with impatience since, as you cannot fail to know, I am very attached to you. As for myself, I can report that it is now more than three weeks since I arrived here; I found everyone in good health and I myself am well. You know, I am quite inactive here, and keep on remembering life at Spasskoye, in particular those days which you spent with us. I keep remembering our talks and that—do you remember, or do you perhaps not wish to remember?—that radiant, burning kiss which suffused my whole being at dinner on the balcony—and so on and so on.

From all this you may draw your own conclusion that you ought not to leave me without a line about yourself. Well, we shall see!

For the present, I kiss your hands and remain

Your loving Ivan Turgenev.

P.S. Have you seen the Polonskys? Even they do not write anything about you. Apparently, "different days, different dreams". *Dreams* wouldn't be such a serious matter, but deeds . . .[58]

[Turgenev here quotes from Pushkin's *Eugene Onegin*.]

(Bougival, 10 October 1881)
Dear Marya Gavrilovna,

I wrote to you out of turn the day before yesterday, and now I have another chance of talking to you. You have written me such a good letter, so very warm and friendly. I was gladdened by the sight of your handwriting—as beautiful, subtle and fascinating as your hands which are so delightful to kiss. I was sorry to hear that things are not going so well with you as I should have wished, though the only thing that is really bad is the lack of interesting parts. Another matter of regret is that you are not taking care of your health. As for the appointment of M. Vsevolozhsky and all the gossip about your marriage—I shouldn't worry! With regard to the marriage itself, it is too late to ask for my opinion. "Le vin est tiré—il faut le boire"; and to draw back now after all that you have agreed—or allowed to happen—is already impossible. Strange! Last year, when ... well, you know what was happening to me ... I did not give a moment's thought to your marriage—it was simply not in the picture. Now, however, I often wonder about it, probably because my attachment to you is firmer. There is no doubt that you are prompted to this action by a kind of "point d'honneur". Your position will become more correct—or regular—but at the same time more dependent. And in the end you will link your destiny with that of a man with whom, so far as I can judge, you have little in common. In any case, I hope that you will stand up for your freedom as an artist. For you, this is as vital as the air you breathe and you must not allow anyone to stifle you. It would all make sense if there were any strong passion, but there seems to be none. By the way, has the Oranienbaum fancy *completely* melted away?

I was very pleased to read your mention of Spasskoye and your visit there. But why should it not be repeated next year? I shall spend the summer there again. Or will your future husband forbid it? And the Polonskys will probably be there too. By the way, what kind of love are you referring to? I am at a loss to understand you. Can it be that you suspected Zhosefina Antonovna?

I intend to arrive in Petersburg at the beginning of March, after Marianne's confinement (as you see, the young couple have lost no time!)—and by the middle of April I shall go to the country.

The weather is still magnificent, but I read that in Petersburg you have cold and snow. Is it true that you are living in a small flat while Nikita Nikitich spends the winter in Perm, or is he coming to Petersburg? It would seem that he ought at present to be near the Court.

When are you going to act in the part of Glafira?

Well, adieu, my dear, clever girl. At the end of your letter you say that you kiss me affectionately. If it is as it was on the balcony at Spasskoye, my head will start spinning even at a distance of 3000 versts.

Keep well and gay, and let me kiss you.

Your sincere friend, Ivan Turgenev.[59]

[The Vsevolozhsky referred to in this letter was the uncle of Savina's second husband and had just been made Director of all the Imperial theatres. Turgenev did not in fact return to Russia the following summer, or ever again; he was too ill in 1882 and died the next year.]

(Bougival, 30 October 1881)
Dear Marya Gavrilovna,

How pleased I am to get your letters! The sight of your handwriting alone gladdens me! I feel that you are honest with me and trust me and I feel too that I am very much attached to you. I am *very* sorry that I do not see you and will not be seeing you soon—not earlier than March. Now you are dreaming about quietly slipping off abroad. For my part, I am dreaming how good it would be to travel about—just the two of us—for at least a month, and in such a way that no one would know who or where we were. And afterwards we should each return to our respective work—or idleness! Probably this would not give you much pleasure—but I should be happy. (You too, perhaps—who knows?) Both your dreams and mine will, beyond question, remain dreams. But my imagination cannot help painting pleasant pictures. For me, old man that I am, it is enough.

With all my heart I wish you a good and interesting role. The lack of one to which you could devote your natural creative talent must inevitably make you feel depressed. (Not to speak of the uncertain position with regard to Nikita Nikitich, from which it seems you cannot escape.) That you are highly gifted as an artist was proved to me by your extraordinary story about your antics at Oranienbaum. You related it all so passionately, subtly and *naïvely* that you misled even an old bird like me because you yourself were in the net. But in truth, was it really like that? What would have happened if the "object" had suddenly appeared? What kind of *move* would have followed? Would it have been an immediate *checkmate*? My dear, don't be cross: your little hand, please, and I will kiss its back and its palm.

I read in the papers that performances have been cancelled during the great fast, by order of the Reverend Pobedonostsev. This would be a time to seize the chance and be off abroad! I myself may just manage to get to Petersburg.

It is wrong of you not to have visited the Polonskys; they are good people, and they like you. And why on earth was I not in the shoes of Yakov Petrovich when he so successfully caught sight of you in the bath-house? But that's the way of it—I was born a Simple Simon and I shall remain one.

You write that you have a small flat; but do you receive lots of people? I don't mean the admirers and worshippers—who are *les intimes*?

Who is the one who does not allow you to be bored? In this respect I suppose—you see, I have a good opinion of myself!—that no one can replace me completely.

Just imagine the following picture. Venice (perhaps in October, the best month in Italy) or Rome. Two foreigners in travelling clothes—one tall, clumsy, white-haired, long-legged, but very contented: the other a slender lady with remarkable dark eyes and black hair. Let us suppose her contented as well. They walk about the town, ride in gondolas. They visit galleries, churches and so on, they dine together in the evening, they are at the theatre together—and then? There my imagination stops respectfully. Is it in order to conceal something, or because there is nothing to conceal?

What nonsense I am writing! All my friends here leave for

Paris next week; I shall stay on for another ten days, in complete solitude. I want to try to do some work.

And now (after all, no one will see this letter?) I take your dear little head between both my hands and kiss your lips—this delightful fresh rose—and imagine how the rose burns and quivers under my caresses. Do I imagine—or do I remember?

Your Ivan Turgenev.[60]

[The bath-house episode which Turgenev mentions ruefully here caused Savina some distress. In December 1883, after Turgenev was dead, she wrote to Polonsky's wife about it:

"I could not sleep all night, remembering our conversation yesterday evening. Perhaps, however, I misunderstood you when you said that, in his reminiscences of Spasskoye, Yakov Petrovich described the episode in the bath-house. You know how wicked people are and how many enemies I have. Also, my relationship with Ivan Sergeyevich has always been interpreted in the nastiest, dirtiest way, and so of course something filthy will be made out of this trivial episode. Will it be pleasant to read the sneering remarks of some nonentity? Certainly not for me, and not for Yakov Petrovich either. For goodness' sake, persuade him against it—and for my sake, and above all in respect for the memory of Ivan Sergeyevich."[61]

Polonsky must have agreed with Savina, for the episode does not appear in his published memoirs.

In the winter of 1881 Savina went to Kiev for a rest from the theatre. On 8 December there was a disastrous fire at the Vienna Ring Theatre, to which Turgenev refers in his next letter:]

(Paris, 15 December 1881)
Dear Marya Gavrilovna,

I have been waiting for you to reply to my last letter; but the recent references in the papers to your health began to worry me. Now I learn from Toporov that you have been obliged to go away and that you left your address with him for me to write to you. This made me very unhappy—although I hope that your illness is not at all dangerous and that you will soon return to the stage—but all the same, this isn't good. I shall get to Petersburg by the beginning of *April* and of course I will find you already there. Now, please don't be too lazy to write to me from Kiev about how you are and what you are doing. This must have been the reason why you gave Toporov your address. Surely there is no need to repeat what you already know perfectly—namely, how well I love you.

As for myself, I can tell you that I am as fit as a fiddle and have even started to do a bit of work. By the way, did you expect my "Song" to be such a success? I for one didn't expect it. I am awaiting the confinement of my dear Marianne—so far everything is going fine; she is now in her eighth month. I am annoyed with my compatriots who behave so foolishly over the intolerable Sarah Bernhardt. She has nothing to boast of but a charming voice—everything else in her is falsehood, coldness, affectation—and a repulsive Parisian swank. This charlatan, this publicity-seeker, has taken the absurd step of wiring—she herself, you understand!—all the newspapers about how the firemen rescued *her* things from the unfortunate theatre. What do you think of that? A thousand people perish—let them! It seems that so long as Sarah's things are saved there is no need to grieve over anything else. This kind of thing makes the ancient blood of my serf-owning ancestors stir in me. Honestly, I could whip this buffoon of a woman with my own hands—only, it's a pity she is so thin! Please excuse this rather vulgar fooling! Let us see how the Petersburg critics treat this lady.

And so, *be sure* to write—and *soon*, otherwise I shall be cross with you and not want to kiss your hands, even in my imagination. No, nonsense, I shall always want to kiss them, and not only them, but...

"Never mind, never mind, just keep silent," as Gogol says. But do write.

Yours, Ivan Turgenev.[62]

(Paris, 21 December 1881)
Dear Marya Gavrilovna,

Your letter from Kiev arrived today, which is the 9th according to our Russian calendar, and you write that you will be leaving on the 15th. My reply will scarcely reach you in Kiev. I could almost be pleased by this, for your departure would show that your health has improved. (Incidentally, I wrote to you about a week ago and I hope that you have received that letter.) Today, therefore, I am sending you only a few lines—in order to thank you for remembering me, to wish you the best of everything, especially peace of mind—and also, since I need not be so wary of expressing my feelings as you must, to kiss your charming hands in my imagination. By the way, I must point out to you that a fair dose of feminine cruelty is needed to write, as you did, the words in answer to the advice of your friends—"I replied with great regret that it was quite impossible to follow these suggestions". But cruelty too becomes you—that is how fate ordains it.

And so, au revoir—in Petersburg, in March. I cannot possibly be earlier. I have no doubt of finding you in the full bloom of health and strength and I hope to get the kiss which you have "saved up" for me and which will, perhaps, recall the one that almost burned me on the balcony at Spasskoye.

Yours, Ivan Turgenev.[63]

[Turgenev affected indifference about Savina's impending marriage to Vsevolozhsky, but he was in fact aggrieved and

almost bitter about it. He revealed something of his true feelings in a letter to Polonsky's wife on 1 January 1882:
"... I received a letter from Savina, from Kiev. It seems that she had gone there to take a short rest and improve her health. But who can really make her out? It is hard to imagine anyone feeling the absence of a man like Vsevolozhsky. However, he is handsome and is, so far as one knows, capable of loving her—two qualities which women like, or so we are assured by experts of the human heart."][64]

(Paris, 10 January 1882)
Dear Marya Gavrilovna,
I learn from the papers that you have returned to Petersburg and from Toporov that he has seen you and that apparently your health is completely restored. I send my congratulations on that account, and also New Year greetings. Perhaps in the course of this year your life will be finally settled and you will calm down and rest. I have often thought about you all this time—more often than I should—because I am very attached to you and shall be very glad to see you. This cannot be before the end of March, as Marianne's confinement will not be before the end of February. Will your benefit performance take place soon? What kind of play is to be put on for it? What role have you been playing recently, and how did the public receive you? You haven't changed your Petersburg flat? According to you it is too small, so it is bound to be crowded for two—and you told Zhosefina Antonovna that you were longing for Nikita Nikitich, so you will probably ask him to join you. You see how many questions I am putting to you. I kiss your little right hand, and ask it not to be too lazy but to give me the answers.
As for myself, I can report that I am well. I cannot say that I am feeling depressed, though I am in a sort of stupor. By the way, I am nevertheless writing something [probably *Clara*

Milich]. Not a comedy as the papers reported. Alas, I am not good at that, otherwise what a part I should have devised for you! In Petersburg, perhaps you will come over for tea in the evenings as you did last year, and I will tell you some of my thoughts and you will talk to me as you did at Spasskoye. I expect that you will have a lot to tell me—I only hope that there will be nothing that you want to keep to yourself.

They say that the weather in Petersburg is nasty at present: take care not to become ill again. Did you get the letter which I sent to Kiev?

I kiss your delightfully clever forehead and remain,
your friend Ivan Turgenev.

P.S. One more question—but this really is the last—did you stay in Moscow for another few days as you thought you might, and did you see Fedotova [a famous actress]? Did you admire her?[65]

(Paris, 21 January 1882)

Thank you, delightful kitten, for your delightful letter. Your little paw, please. I kiss it all over, very tenderly. I am very happy about your successes—both present and future— and I cannot help scolding you because *vous vous laissez brouter*. I mentioned it to a Frenchwoman who is being exploited just as you are. She laughed and remarked that *il n'y a que les animaux qui broutent*. I see that my letter to Grigorovich has raised a whole storm in the dirty tea-cup of our national press. He acted very indiscreetly in making this letter known— but I would not withdraw my opinion expressed in it about Sarah Bernhardt, which is, by the way, well known to you. If you had her voice—well, she would be unworthy to wash your feet, and not only because washing your little feet would be a very pleasant occupation. And it is not my fault that the horrid Suvorin happened to be right this time.

You have answered my questions very sweetly, and now all

I have to do is wait—impatiently—until you tell me everything "over a cup of tea". I know that you are sincere and that you trust me, for which I am deeply grateful. Be sure to write to me the day after your benefit night—at least two words—at least one. And because the public loves you and gives you such a reception, I call the public a pet and stroke its head.

You ask me what makes me think that your forehead is so charmingly intelligent. Good heavens—it's my own observation. After all, I have eyes! You think that an intelligent forehead must be open and high? On the contrary, an intelligent female forehead must be of medium size, a little bit sloping, a little bit uneven, with pale, delicate hollows above the brows, slightly rounded towards the temples, luminous at times—well, that is just how yours is. But then everything of yours is intelligent, but also... But you know all this yourself. "Il y a une vraie artiste dans ces yeux-là" was the comment made to me by one lady—a good judge of these things—when she looked at your photograph.

Your uncertain position has still not been clarified. But, my dear, it ought to be clarified, if only for the sake of your own career. Perhaps you will succeed in doing so this year? You wish me "all the best" for this year: "all the best" is a very accommodating phrase and I am making it include all kinds of unattainable things... and on my part I wish you a solution to your uncertainty in this same year. We shall talk about all this.

Well, now—out of all this admiring crowd which has received and surrounded you, has not a new, desperate admirer come forward? And what about last year's railway man; hasn't he emerged from the obscurity into which he vanished? I can't imagine you forgoing the pleasure of "pushing off" those who push themselves. Or is it that you cannot be bothered, especially with your benefit performance so near at hand?

You conclude your letter by returning my kiss "with the Spasskoye kiss added". Do you know what it feels like to receive such a kiss? An overwhelming desire to fall down at the feet of the giver ... so you can picture the humble position in which I take leave of you.

Keep well and gay and cheerful, my dear, my love, and believe in the sincere feelings of,

your friend Ivan Turgenev.[66]

[Turgenev did not write again until March. In the meantime he had been suffering from personal worries, especially over his illegitimate daughter Paulinette Bruère. Her mother, a seamstress at Spasskoye, was turned out by Turgenev's mother when the child was born. Turgenev made arrangements for her to live in Moscow while the little girl, christened Pelageya, stayed at Spasskoye. Turgenev's mother treated her badly, sometimes as a member of the family and sometimes as a servant according to the whim of the moment. At last Turgenev sent her to France, where she was brought up by Pauline Viardot with her own children and lost all traces of her Russian origin. He had little affection for her, but his sense of duty made him ensure that she lacked nothing. It was in fact the substantial settlement that he made on her which attracted Gaston Bruère. When the marriage turned out badly, Turgenev made fresh provision for her, even selling his horses and pictures in order to send her to Switzerland.

There was another worry, too, foreshadowed in the half-jocular remark of the previous letter about the "railway man" —probably Vyshnegradsky, a director of the south-western railways. Now comes the first mention of a much more serious rival for Savina's affection—the "immortal warrior" Skobolev, a general who had taken part in the Russo-Turkish war of 1877–8. Savina wrote the word "Yes" by Turgenev's question about his name.]

(Paris, 14 March 1882)

Dear Marya Gavrilovna,

I was so glad to get your letter although it caught me in the worst possible mood. My old friend Viardot almost died two weeks ago and is still in bed and not out of danger. In addition, my daughter with her two children was forced to leave her husband, who had completely ruined her, had taken to drink and was running round with a revolver in his hand—and so on. I had to help her to get away.

But, to make up for all this, Marianne after a difficult confinement gave birth to a little girl; mother and child are now doing well. You can imagine how happy I am. I shall never forget the movingly blissful look on her face the day after the confinement; such beauty is given to a woman only once in a lifetime.

I wrote just now that I was glad to receive your letter, but its bad news about your health grieved me. They say that Meran is a charming place; try to spend some time there—say, at least a month—in complete solitude. And if you are bored and irritable, it won't matter: a great doctor used to say that anger and boredom in a patient are sure signs of recovery.

Let your imagination have full rein ... and it certainly must be a vivid one if you could meet a man in Russia—a military man at that—who has so impressed and charmed you that you doubt whether he is mortal! Is it Skobolev by any chance?

I shall be very glad to listen to your "confession" at Spasskoye, if only you will go there. I hope to extricate myself from Paris at the end of April; I shall be at Spasskoye from 10 May to 10 September. The Polonskys will be there as well. By the way, Zhosefina Antonovna has told me again that you are eager to be with Nikita Nikitich and that you feel assured of marrying him this year; well and good, but how does this tie up with the phenomenal warrior? Let us assume that you feel nothing but goodwill for him; but even this feeling, if it is strong enough, can drive out all the rest. However, I will put off this discussion until we can chat together in my old-fashioned study—or in the garden, on the little bench in front of my favourite twin silver fir.

All that you write to me about your ovations in Petersburg and the public's love for you does not surprise me in the least. It would be difficult not to love you—I know this from my own experience.

I am sorry you have not been able to get a good part this year. I repeat for the hundredth time, why am I not a playwright? A delightful figure has matured in my mind; but how to give it action, what kind of plot to invent—that is not my line. Incidentally, about the theatre—I don't remember whether I have told you that I wrote to Davydov about his success in *The Bachelor*. I received a very nice and clever reply from him, full of great appreciation for you. I should very much like to see Davydov on the stage.

And Grigorovich too wrote to me about you. Although he is a bit of a *windbag* I feel that he is attached to you—I have the right nose for it. In spite of certain failings which are inherent in our human nature, he is an excellent person and a *true friend*.

For all my troubles, my health remains satisfactory and I wish I could share it with you—that at least, for I have little chance of sharing anything else.

For the first time, you have not considered me worthy of a kiss. *Immortal* warrior, you are behind it all! Nevertheless, I am so bold when saying good-bye as to kiss your forehead if everything else is inaccessible.

Be sure not to leave me without news of you; and above all, get well, rest and please—be angry, even if it is with me—but believe that, in whatever trouble I may find myself, I shall always remain your true friend, more true than Grigorovich or whoever else.

Yours, Ivan Turgenev.[67]

(Paris, 25 March 1882)
Dear Marya Gavrilovna,

You are thanking me for my letter, and I am thanking you for yours. So you are bored and melancholy—that is not too serious! "Boredom is rest for the soul", as Pushkin says [*Scenes from Faust*], and melancholy is only for the young who still have much ahead of them. This state of melancholy is like a bird which cannot yet fly wherever it wishes, though the wings are there—and what strong ones!—so that it will fly in time.

But that your health is not fully restored is a bad thing. What is the climate of Meran doing about it? I hope it will soon remember its duty and that you will fully recover. Your description of Meran is delightful and detailed—but I could not help smiling, just to myself. Discoursing on the beauties of Meran you have found it possible not to mention one word about that amazing warrior who made such a great impression on you, and you have said nothing about your matrimonial plans. But please don't think that I want to worm myself importunately into your secrets. I feel only gratitude—both for your promise to stay with me at Spasskoye and for that two-fold kiss which you so graciously sent me.

I assume that my letter will still catch you at Meran; I entirely approve of your intention of going to Italy, particularly to Florence. I spent ten of the most delightful days in Florence, many, many years ago. Florence left on me the most fascinating and poetic impression—even though I was there *alone*. What would it have been like, had I been in the company of a woman who was understanding, good and beautiful—that above all! At that time I was still under forty. A respectable age . . . yet I was still young—not the ruin I am now.

But the past cannot be restored. Should you find yourself in Florence, give her my regards. Amid her wonders I bore a heart in love, but a love without an object. No, it's not true: I was in love with Florence. Oh, those beauties in stone!

You are a beauty, though not in stone; but it is not by my rays that you are made warm. You need a warrior—and a young one and an *immortal* one. What can I say to that? You are right.

But the kiss permit me to return—to the eyes that sent it and the hand that has written about it.

Your friend Ivan Turgenev.[68]

[Meran did not fulfil the hopes which Turgenev had placed on it and Savina came to Paris for consultations about her health. Turgenev arranged for her first of all to see a Doctor Hirtz but she felt no confidence in his treatment. Turgenev had been receiving advice on his own deteriorating condition from the great Charcot, at this time at the height of his fame as a neurologist, who he hoped might be able to help Savina. The correspondence in the spring of 1882 tells its own sad story of illness and concern.]

(Paris, 31 March 1882)
Dear Marya Gavrilovna,

It was not until 9 o'clock that I got your note inviting me to visit you between 4 and 7, so I couldn't carry out your wish. I shall come tomorrow (Saturday) at 1 o'clock, and shall be at your service. I am happy that we are about to meet again, but the thought that it is illness which has brought you here saddens me. However, we shall talk about all this, and for the time being I kiss your hands and remain,

Yours, Ivan Turgenev.[69]

(Paris, 2 April 1882)
Dear Marya Gavrilovna,
 Yesterday I asked Hirtz to visit you this morning before 12 o'clock, so you should wait in for him.
 Yours, I.T.[70]

(Same day)
Dear Marya Gavrilovna,
 I can't manage to call on you today at 2 o'clock. I shall drop in at 5 to find out the result of your meeting with the doctor. Should you have to go out at that time, leave a short note.
 Yours, Ivan Turgenev.[71]

(Same day—to Madame Polonskaya)
Dear Zhosefina Antonovna,
 Savina arrived here three days ago, for a consultation with Charcot. She intends to go to Spasskoye as well—but it is difficult to count on her visit with certainty.[72]

(Paris, 3 April 1882)
Dear Marya Gavrilovna,
 I shall be at your place at 11.30. Although the doctor has tired you out, I am glad that he did not find any serious illness. You can trust him—he is most reliable.
 See you soon.
 Yours, I.T.[73]

(Paris, 4 April 1882)
Dear Marya Gavrilovna,
 If that's the way it is—and you are willing to have a talk with Charcot—then let's drop Hirtz. I am vexed as you are—even more so. I am not at all well today but I shall most certainly see you.
 Yours, Ivan Turgenev.[74]

(Paris, 10 April 1882—to Toporov)

M. G. Savina is here at present, and receiving treatment from Charcot. Her illness may be serious—but there is no danger...[75]

(Same day—to Grigorovich)

M. G. Savina arrived here about a week ago and is receiving treatment from Charcot. She is seriously, but not dangerously, ill...[76]

(Paris, 11 April 1882)
Dear Marya Gavrilovna,

I am still unwell, but shall be at your place at 1 o'clock. Don't worry any more about Hirtz. I'll make arrangements to get rid of him and you will not see his face again.

All yours, I.T.[77]

(Same day)
Dear Marya Gavrilovna,

Such an attack of neuralgia hit me that I had to take some medicine and must stay at home, so I cannot come to you at 1 o'clock. I hope that you at least are keeping your chin up. Should you be at home tonight, I might summon up my strength and crawl over to you at 9 o'clock for a cup of tea.

Let me know, in two words.

Yours, Ivan Turgenev.[78]

This is the note I wrote you half an hour ago, and then yours arrived. That's how les beaux esprits se rencontrent. It's a pity that it is due to ill health; but if I am up and about, I'll appear at your house at 9 o'clock.

Yours, I.T.

[Turgenev managed to get there and Savina still remembered the evening eleven years later, when she described it to Bazilevsky:]

... I can see it as if it were today—the venerable figure of Ivan Sergeyevich, who came to see me on April 11th with a small pot of the most wonderful azaleas in each hand and wishing me "to bloom as they bloom".[79]

(Same day—Madame Polonskaya)
M. G. Savina is here, receiving treatment. I do not often see her, but she is as nice as ever [*some words are here crossed out*] her health is not so bad as people in Russia believe...[80]

(to Hirtz)
Monsieur le docteur,
Etant obligée de quitter Paris, Madame Savina m'a chargé de vous prier de m'envoyer la note des visites que vous lui avez faites. Je vous les payerai immédiatement.
Recevez l'assurance de ma considération très distinguée.
Ivan Tourguéneff.[81]

(Paris, 17 April 1882)
I am not at all well, dear Marya Gavrilovna. I am going to Charcot today at 3 o'clock, but shall be with you at 1.30.
I kiss your hands.
Yours, I.T.[82]

(Paris, 18 April 1882)
Dear Marya Gavrilovna,
Charcot has definitely diagnosed my illness as angine de poitrine and has forbidden me to leave my room for about ten days. And so, whoever wants to see me...
How is your health? You gave me great happiness yesterday.
Yours, I.T.[83]

[Savina was alarmed by the mention of *angina*—which in Russian can mean "tonsillitis"—and was afraid to visit in case of infection.]

(Paris, 19 April 1882)
Dear Marya Gavrilovna,

Angine de poitrine has nothing in common with the ordinary angine. This is a neuralgic heart disease—a very painful one—but there is no question of infection. The term (angine) is used here in the Latin sense of "suffering". But you were right not to come, as you yourself are still out of sorts. And I am worse today. I shall have to put off the pleasure of seeing you and kissing you (which is quite harmless—in every respect) until we next meet.

For the time being I kiss your hands.
Yours, I.T.[84]

(Paris, 1 May 1882)
Dear Marya Gavrilovna,

I don't like to make reproaches, but all the same I am cross that you are not taking care of yourself—driving out at night and so on. I sympathize with you very much—but I hope you will soon be better. As for myself, my illness may not be too serious, but it is incurable. I have to keep in the same ridiculous position. My stupid condition is showing no change.

I kiss your hands and remain
Yours, I.T.[85]

(Paris, 8 May 1882)
Dear Marya Gavrilovna,

My condition is just the same—but if you are feeling well, stay at home. I am sending you the volume with *Asya*.

I kiss you with fatherly tenderness.
Yours, I.T.[86]

(Same day)
Dear Marya Gavrilovna,

It's a pity you do not listen to me—so you are unwell. As for me, everything is unchanged, or even a bit worse. I kiss you in expectation of a meeting. But do not come if it upsets you.

Yours, I.T.[87]

(Same day)

I shall be expecting you, dear Marya Gavrilovna; but I am still very unwell.

Yours, I.T.[88]

[Sadness and resignation appear increasingly in the letters he wrote at this time. Even a brief selection from his extensive correspondence reveals how he was suffering—difficulty in walking, standing, even breathing, with sharp pains in his shoulder and chest. He realized that he might never see Russia again, but his longing to be at Spasskoye grew stronger up to the day he died and he refused to give up hope.]

(Paris, 20 May 1882—to Madame Polonskaya)

... It seems that my illness is taking a turn for the better. Today I could get up—with two people helping me, it's true. I could sit in the armchair for about a quarter of an hour and managed to stand for about two minutes, which is particularly important. My gout is receding and the pain in the shoulder and chest has abated. I hope that in two weeks they will take me to Bougival—and then, who knows? In a month or six weeks we'll be off to Spasskoye! To live at least for a little while as last year. But it's still early to indulge in these hopes.[89]

(Paris, 26 May 1882—to Tolstoy)

... The main trouble is that, through failing to respond very well to drugs, this illness can last a long time. And having deprived me of freedom of movement, it makes my going to Spasskoye more remote—indefinitely so. How I've planned that trip, how I've looked forward to it! But all hope is not yet lost ... as for the question of remaining alive, I shall probably live for a long time, though my race is run.[90]

(Paris, 4 June 1882—to Madame Polonskaya)

... tomorrow they are taking me to Bougival, as my health has not improved here—on the contrary, it has recently become worse ...[91]

(Bougival, 8 June 1882—to the same)

... and all round me, everything is green and blossoming, the birds are singing and so on. But all this is fine and delightful when one is well; now I cannot help remembering "heartless nature" ...[92]

[By this time Savina had finished her treatment with Charcot and had gone back to the estate of her future husband at Siva, where she stayed until September. Even Turgenev had not guessed that she was waiting so eagerly for the Russian spring to begin; she recalled her experience in a letter to Bazilevsky from Petersburg, 19 April 1893:]

At the first news that the ice on the Volga was moving, I left for Russia—rightly believing that I should find it warmer and healthier at Siva than in alien Sicily. I travelled for ten days without stopping. After driving by coach for about 93 versts along a road which the thaw had made terrible, I changed my travelling-clothes and went, as if nothing had happened, to look at the house and garden. The garden! The trees were bare but each of them had a small wooden box for starlings—and how those starlings sang! By the window of my room the birdcherry was bursting into bloom—and with what scent! In some places there was still snow, but the brooks were running so gaily and noisily, the sun was shining so brightly, and I felt such a warmth. Since then I have never believed in journeys abroad; I know what "spring" is like. I do not know any greater poetry than the poetry of the countryside.[93]

(Bougival, 7 June 1882)
Dear Marya Gavrilovna,

Yesterday they partly carried and partly drove me here. It goes without saying that my first desire is to write to you at the address which you left me. However, don't let this move make you suppose that my health has greatly improved. The doctors set hopes on a change of air—that's all. I am beginning to feel convinced that it is impossible for me to get completely well and that I shall never be able to stand, walk and so forth as ordinary people do. This illness is one of those from which many artists, writers and other hypersensitive people tend to suffer at the age of sixty. It sticks to them, like a faithful wife, until the end of their days. One must reconcile oneself, though it is not easy to do so. If only this illness had waited for another brief year I should have managed to go to Spasskoye—and so on, and so on. I have made so many plans, literary and business ones, and plans of all sorts! Now all this has melted away, and I am totally extinguished. My only comfort is that those whom I dearly love are *well* and that you occupy one of the foremost places among them—you, of course, do not doubt it. To give more conviction to your being *well*—as soon as you get this letter take your pen and write me a few lines to say where you are, and how things are with you—and what life is like for you. You will give me much joy by doing this. For the time being I am alone here, but the Viardot family will arrive soon. To make sure that I get your letter, you had better address it to 50, Rue de Douai.

If I am much better I will write to you; otherwise I'll wait for your reply.

With all my heart I wish you health, happiness and peace of mind—and I kiss your charming hands with great tenderness.

Your decrepit but truly devoted friend,
Ivan Turgenev.[94]

(Bougival, 19 June 1882)
Dear Marya Gavrilovna,

Your letter from Siva fell on my grey life like a rose petal on the surface of a muddy stream. The move here from Paris has not brought the expected change for the better. On the contrary, my health has considerably deteriorated and now I am in the condition that I was on the day you came to say goodbye. I can just manage to walk—the gout in my feet has gone. But the pains in my chest and shoulder have increased and I'm almost condemned to immobility—I can't raise my hands as far as my face, and so on. I don't know if all this is caused by the nasty, damp weather which has hung on since my move here (it will soon be two weeks!) or if my illness is an incurable one—I am almost convinced that it is. In any case, the fact remains. My spirits are gone; I try not to look too far ahead into the future and I no longer allow myself to dream about seeing you again. Instead I am happy with all my heart—as far as is possible for a man who is only half alive—that you are all right and that you are resting both emotionally and physically. As for your plans (those for your marriage and other things) I am certain that you have enough sense and intelligence to make the right decision. You did well to sign the contract for two years. When does it take effect? From September?

With regard to my letters to you—you can do as you please with them. The same thing as you would have done with me, if only... if only... I leave it to you to finish the sentence. I know for certain that when I am talking to you in my letters, it is to you alone; but, even without your knowledge, a strange hand may one day touch these pages... Still, this is all nonsense, and I repeat: do as you think fit.

My dear friend, I have grown so subdued that I do not permit myself to ponder the meaning of these words in your letter—"Do remember sometimes how difficult it was for me to say goodbye to you in Paris, and *what my feelings were then*". I know for certain that, if our lives had crossed earlier ... but what is the point of all this? Like Lemm, my German character in *A Nest of Gentlefolk*, I look into the grave and not into a rosy future.

Forgive me for writing such sad things to you, but I find it impossible to pretend to you. Remember how through it all there runs just one thing only: that I love you very, very much.

You have not written me anything about the "warrior". What about him? Has he turned up again in Petersburg? I hope you managed to deal with him. And what about some new parts for you? It still seems to me that you have not yet found a playwright who is truly worthy of you. You have probably flitted through Moscow without seeing anyone there. (You probably know that poor Maslov has recovered but is no better than an idiot through softening of the brain.) And have you seen Strepetova in the role of Mary Stuart? (!!!?!)

Well, goodbye, my dear. Do write to me at least once more from far away. And I kiss a thousand times your hands—and everything that you will allow me to kiss—and remain for ever,

Your faithful friend Ivan Turgenev.[95]

[Soon after Savina's death, Filosofov gave her account of how she visited Turgenev during his last illness. When she described old Viardot's entry, Savina jumped up and imitated his rumbling voice.]

Turgenev—already almost dying. In Paris. The room is upstairs. Small, with a low ceiling. Downstairs is the flat occupied by the Viardot family. The monotonous scales and runs can be heard. Mme Viardot is giving a lesson. Someone knocks at the door. Old Viardot enters to visit his friend: "I shall never forget this terrible scene. Our Turgenev, our pride, so neglected and so lonely."[96]

(Bougival, 9 July 1882)

We exchange our letters almost across half the globe, dear Marya Gavrilovna! I am very happy to learn that my letters give you some pleasure: yours are a great comfort to me in my miserable condition. But today I am particularly sad: yesterday I learned of Skobolev's death. At first I could not believe that our Achilles had perished so early, betraying the hopes of all those who had foretold a great future for him. I do not idly compare him to Achilles, for that young man too was snatched away by death—as was Alexander of Macedonia. Russia is unfortunate in her great ones. The Russian people, in whose eyes he was the most popular figure of the day—and whose grief will be immense and general—will scarcely believe that he died from natural causes. I should not be surprised to hear of his bitterest enemies, the Germans at Court, suffering an attack even worse than the Jews often receive. But enough of all this.

I can tell by the tone of your letter that you are all right at Siva, and I am happy with all my heart. You have uttered no word either of your marriage or of Nikita Nikitich. Meanwhile, it appears from the papers that the whole estate of Nikita Nikitich has been bought by Demidov-San-Donato. Is this true? If so, is there anything to prevent his living where you will be—I mean, in Petersburg? Or perhaps Demidov has bought only the factories and the estate itself (Siva) will remain in the hands of Nikita Nikitich. Please clear all this up for me.

As for myself—no change whatever has taken place in my illness, and none can do so; for, according to the doctor's verdict, this illness is one of those which are incurable. I am trying to get used to this idea; and sometimes I comfort myself with the thought that I might have gone blind like a friend of mine—the brilliant General Engelhardt to whom this happened suddenly. This too is incurable, but a thousand times worse. At least I can believe that some day—when?—I don't know—I may be able to see your dear face.

Of course, I shall not get to Spasskoye this year—perhaps not to Russia either. All the Polonskys have now gathered at Spasskoye. Zhosefina Antonovna keeps on writing cordial letters and urging me to go there, saying how well everything is now arranged, how everyone is waiting for me and what wonderful weather they are having. But here it continues to be dreadful—rain and cold. Yesterday and today we had the fires lit—just think of that! To make up for this, we have all come together now and are all well. This too is a great comfort. I should not grumble at all if it were not for the nights—agonizing, sleepless nights.

Without having any special practical reason for it—I should be grateful if you wrote to tell me exactly when—that is, on what date—you are leaving Siva, when you will arrive in Moscow, and eventually in Petersburg. Will you be acting in Moscow?

Goodbye, my dear friend; I kiss your charming hands many times and ask you not to forget

Your ailing old friend I.T.[97]

P.S. Once you promised to send me the plaster cast of your hand. Have you forgotten—or has one not yet been made? I remind you, just in case.

[A cast was in fact made and is now in the Leningrad State Theatre Museum. Although Turgenev tried to keep a cheerful tone in his letter to Savina, he was suffering a great deal. The sudden death of Skobolev at the age of thirty-nine was a shock which added depression to his physical illness. He was more outspoken to other correspondents, as for instance to Zhosefina Antonovna Polonskaya:]

I assure you that if I don't write more frequently it is only in order not to distress you more frequently. There is no change in my condition: the illness is like a granite rock. At times it seems to be slightly better, then it gets worse again. Here is my daily timetable at present. The nights are usually bad; I keep on waking in spite of hot compresses, chloroform and even morphia. The pains are particularly sharp between three and seven in the morning. The later morning is usually quieter; I can stand and walk, only for a short time of course, and with mechanical aid. Without this aid, any movement is unthinkable. Towards dinner, the *right* shoulder-blade begins to ache and the pain grows sharper and more tormenting up to ten o'clock. Writing aggravates the pain (because of the movement of the hand). It is obviously hopeless to think of travel. So be good and don't encourage me to come to Spasskoye, don't say how I should recover there, how everyone would look after me, and so on. I know all this perfectly well, but it only makes things harder for me. I try to reconcile myself to my hopeless situation, and therefore make an effort totally to drive away any hopes or dreams for the future. My *personal* life has ceased . . .[98]

(Bougival, 23 July 1882—to Savina)

My dear friend, your (third) letter arrived after some unexplained delay and I received it only yesterday. There is something in this letter for which it is inadequate to kiss your hand without first kneeling down—as I am doing now.

As for my health, I can tell you that it seems to be starting to improve—though I have lost faith and do not allow myself to hope, for the uncertainty of the outcome remains as before and I dare make no assumption. It is not that I think of death—with this kind of illness one can live many long years—but I think that this year I am condemned to immobility and a vegetable existence. But enough of this! What will be, will be, and for the time being there is no point in trying to look into the future.

These last days I feel particularly depressed by the terrible news of the catastrophe on the Kursk line. This horror occurred only a few versts from Spasskoye. The Polonskys, who are now all at Spasskoye, gave me details that made my blood run cold. Nothing like this has happened before. It is possible that a young relative of mine perished in this crash—N. N. Turgenev, a fine fellow whom I saw only last year when he was a student in Moscow. And all these unfortunates suffered martyrdom.

Speaking of death, your hero M. D. Skobolev is no more! Fate does not spare our great Russians—but in this case fate has mocked us cruelly and outrageously. To make this hero die in a brothel! A great and deep sorrow for all Russians.

But what a mournful letter I am writing to you! We should do better to speak about your stage parts. I have no fears for you in the role of the Snowmaiden, although you say that this *poetic* creation does not suit you (why not?) I am convinced that you will be charming in it. But as regards the tragedy in *verse*—you are not so good at reading verse. Do you know why? You read it as if you were afraid of it, and without the naturalness which is characteristic of you. You drop into a rather monotonous sort of voice—what is known as *elocution*. One should be perfectly at ease with verse, (especially verse by Averkiyev) and simply observe the metre without giving unnatural emphasis to the words and so forth. You see, I can be critical even of you. It seems to me that I could be of some use to you if I could read through this part with you. In any case, it would be very pleasant for me to do so. But this, like many other things, must be assigned to the realm of impossible daydreams.

Again you have not told me a word about Nikita Nikitich. I can see from your letter, however, that you had not yet received my *previous* letter and therefore could not reply to several questions which I asked you in it. Also, you tell me nothing about your health; I take this silence as a good sign—it must mean that you are pleased with your health, and this makes me happy.

But it is time to finish. You know beyond doubt that I love you dearly, but it is a pleasure for me to repeat it—and the same pleasure, even if only in imagination, to kiss you with all the tenderness you will allow.

I remain your sincere friend Ivan Turgenev.[99]

[Savina did not, in fact, appear in *The Snowmaiden* by A. N. Ostrovsky, which was first performed in 1900 at the Alexandrinsky Theatre. The "tragedy in verse" refers to *Trogirsky Voyevoda* by D. V. Averkiyev—the part of Zoritsa.]

(Bougival, 8 August 1882)
Dear Marya Gavrilovna,

I have this very minute received your letter of 23 July (it took seventeen days!) and am replying immediately. You complain that it is a long time since I wrote to you—but I always answer regularly; it is the distance! First of all, let me congratulate you not only on your marriage but also on having resolved a false position which was a burden to you. That was precisely what I had in mind when I said that I trust your wisdom. I sincerely wish (and have hope that my wish will be fulfilled) that you will never regret your decision. It could so happen, if Nikita Nikitich were to break his word not to cut short your career as an artist (which, as your husband, he would have a right to do). But Nikita Nikitich is *trop gentleman* for anything of the kind. I thank you too for your detailed replies to my other questions. You are as sweet and charming as ever—and your friend is attached to you *more than ever*.

The condition of this friend continues to be unsatisfactory.

About a week ago they prescribed a milk cure (I am allowed to take nothing but milk). Although it seems that I am a little better and the pain is not so unbearable, the illness itself penetrates me like a nail. To think of going to Russia, even in the autumn, is useless: if I could at least manage to get there in the winter! How happy I shall be to see you in Petersburg! You too will be glad—you see how presumptuous I am!

The Polonskys are living peacefully at Spasskoye and enjoying excellent weather there, while we continue to suffer from cold. Today I almost ordered the fire to be lit. Our young people here have all gone away and only we old ones remain. What's to be done! Everyone has his turn.

I can't even settle down to work. This cursed neuralgia has struck at my very roots. Zhosefina Antonovna, to whom I wrote that I am done for, would not believe me. Alas, I am beginning to think that I am farther gone than I had supposed.

But enough of this sad subject. I am very glad that you do not even mention your health—you must be blossoming and flourishing like a rose. Gather strength for new roles on the stage in the coming season—perhaps I shall be fortunate enough to see you in one of them.

Thank you for your promise to send me the plaster cast of your hand. For the time being, I kiss not the copy but the living hand—and also everything that, in your new position, you will yield to my caresses. Once again I wish you happiness, gaiety and all good things,

Your friend Ivan Turgenev.[100]

P.S. At present I am still addressing my letters to—Savina. How should I write in future?

[Savina had clearly told Turgenev of her impending marriage to N. N. Vsevolozhsky, which took place on 1 August 1882, after a long period of indecision.]

(Bougival, 29 August 1882)
Dear Marya Gavrilovna,

Following the directions in your *fifth* letter I am sending this to Petersburg.

Incidentally, you want to know what phrase I referred to in your *third* letter. Here it is: "Not realizing how boundlessly I adore the wonderful Ivan Sergeyevich". Do you understand that for words such as these one must kneel down at the very least? There is only one fault—since you have forgotten the phrase, you could not have been quite serious in writing it. But then I am not so conceited as to take it literally. For all that, it is still very pleasant.

And so you are in Petersburg again and, from what you say, in the same small flat which I do not know, but hope to come to know in the winter. I rejoice at the good news about your health. And you should not allow anyone to upset it by any sort of intrigue or gossip. Remember what an old family servant once said to me—"Unless a man quarrels with himself, no one can live in peace with him." Don't fret too much!

However unfavourably you speak of your role in *The Snowmaiden*, I should gladly have watched you appearing as an icy little statue. And the burst of passion you would manage—that is certain.

My health is improving with painful slowness. For four weeks now I have been living only on milk—but I see no visible results. Only the nights have become more peaceful. I still stand and walk with great difficulty, but to drive in the carriage is quite impossible. I can barely manage to get to Paris—my chest, back and shoulder start hurting so much. Then how shall I drag myself to Petersburg? But, as you yourself say, there is no point in looking too far ahead.

However, I have taken up literary work again although it progresses very slowly. In all other respects it seems to me that

I have aged by about ten years. Even my resignation is now that of an old man—just to be able to spend the day passably! In addition, the weather here continues to be intolerable. Just imagine, all through the summer we have not stopped heating the rooms; the sky is permanently grey, just like wet linen; rain, wind, damp. There's a heavenly climate for you!

This letter has again turned out to be a sour one. What can I do? If I were not sure of your friendship and understanding, I should not have dared to appear before you in such an unattractive guise. But you must forgive me.

Do write to me from Petersburg. There is no need to tell you how much your letters gladden me. I kiss your dear hands and wish you all the best in the world.

Your friend Ivan Turgenev.

P.S. I am still addressing my letters to "Savina", as you have not given me any different direction.[101]

[Although Turgenev had been able to start work on his last novel, *Clara Milich* (*After Death*), his health was steadily deteriorating. As usual, he felt able to be more open about it to Madame Polonskaya, to whom he wrote on 4 September:]

... I owe you two letters, but the reason for my silence is that I am worse again. To tell you the truth would mean upsetting you, yet I do not want to lie. My illness has become worse; the pains in the right side and shoulder have become considerably sharper; the slightest disturbance brings them on, so that it is impossible for me to drive in the carriage (which previously was possible to some extent). I have to go very cautiously, and that is why I sit or lie down all day long...[102]

[Yet he could still be concerned for other people. His next letter to Savina commended one of Viardot's pupils, who was trying to get an engagement with Josif Yakovlevich Setov, the opera-singer and theatre manager who was for many years in charge of the State theatre at Kiev:]

(Bougival, 9 September 1882)
Dear Marya Gavrilovna,

Today's letter has a special purpose, and that is why I will not tell you about myself. I will say only that the state of my health remains unchanged. Knowing your truly kind heart and your cordial readiness to help, I am turning to you with the following request.

It is about one of Madame Viardot's favourite pupils, a young woman called Vasilenko. She is at present in Kiev and would like to join a theatre company. She has already met M. Setov, who has promised her a début in ten days' time. She is very pretty and graceful, has a beautiful voice (soprano) and sings *excellently*. Above all, her character and intelligence make her worthy of any consideration. I must tell you one thing: Mme Viardot is more attached to her than to any of her other pupils. Vasilenko has all the qualities needed for success, and I do not doubt that she will achieve it. But you know what a letter of recommendation means in this kind of thing, especially from someone like you in the world of the theatre. Besides, I know that you are on friendly terms with Setov and all his family. Drop him a line about this young woman Vasilenko—and I shall take the opportunity to kiss your dear hand again and again. You will be doing something good and useful—not only for the girl. I repeat that she is charming, and if I were thirty and intending to marry I should not choose anyone else—for she is a wonderful housewife in addition to her other virtues. So you will write, won't you, without too much delay.

I have already written to you at your Petersburg flat. You will of course have received it and perhaps you have already been kind enough to reply. So far I have not seen your name in the papers. I kiss you warmly, if you permit me, and very tenderly—if you permit that too. Drop me a line about yourself.

Your devoted friend Ivan Turgenev.[103]

[Savina did what Turgenev asked, and to some effect. The young Vasilenko had been coolly received on her first interview with Setov, but the second time was different:]

... He received me very warmly and even declared that he would like to give me a début performance. As I discovered later, the reason for this startling change in his attitude to me was a letter of recommendation from M. G. Savina ... My début in the role of Margarita passed off very successfully and I was taken into Setov's company.[104]

(Bougival, 18 September 1882)
Dear Marya Gavrilovna,

I recently wrote asking you to intercede with M. Setov on behalf of a good friend of mine, the young woman Vasilenko who is Mme Viardot's pupil. I have no doubt that you have carried out my request because of your friendship for me. But since then I have received a letter from you and of course neither can nor wish to remain in debt to you.

You write that if I came to Petersburg the young people would take great care of me. But what draws me there more strongly is the thought that I might be taking care of you—although, thank God, from what you tell me it seems that you are well and not in need of an old man to be your nursemaid. But there are more ways than one of taking care of you. My way would have been to give myself the pleasure of seeing you, and offering any literary—or other—advice that might be needed. To see you, to talk to you, would be joy indeed. Although the illness is still firmly rooted in me, I refuse to believe that I shall not manage to get to Petersburg, at least by the winter. What delightful—for me—evenings we should spend: just the two of us, without Toporov (to whom, I hasten to add, I am under many obligations but of whom I have no need as a third party). I won't deny that at this very moment—daydreaming and taking advantage of your permission—I am clinging to your adorable little lips, the touch of which can never be forgotten until the end of life—or beyond. [A reminiscence of verses from the poem *Rozmova (The Talk)* by Mizkevich.]

I want to tell you that, thanks to some alleviation of my illness, I have succeeded in writing quite a lengthy novel with a rather venturesome theme. It will probably be published in the January issue of the *European Herald*. How happy I should be if I could read it to you, tête-à-tête. I cannot forget how you listened to me at Spasskoye when I read you an extract from *Spring Torrents* (the tale of Mme Polozova and so on). The plot of this new novel—but no, why should I tell you now? I should like to experience again the sensation which your eyes give me—those eyes fixed on the reader, those glances which burn and soothe at the same time, even when they are not seen and only their radiance can be felt. Well, what will be, will be. There is nothing to be gained by trying to foretell the future.

As the coronation [of Alexander III] has been postponed, you probably did not stop in Moscow; but the papers do not say when you will be making your first appearance. Somehow I cannot imagine any role for you in Fonvizen's *The Ignoramus*. I have not seen you in the title-role of *The Ward*—it's a part that should suit you. And has the author of *The Shy Girl* written nothing this year? It is rumoured that Potekhin has written something. But apparently you are not very pleased with him.

Try to get a little book of tales by Vsevolod Garshin. He is undoubtedly the most talented of our young writers. At present he is living at Spasskoye, together with the family of Zhosefina Antonovna. Yakov Petrovich Polonsky has returned to Petersburg, and I assume that he has seen you. (But not as he did when you were bathing—do you remember? I will never forgive him for that, or rather I will never forgive myself for not having been in his place.)

Adieu, keep well and gay. I kiss your charming hands and everything that you will allow me to kiss.

Your friend Ivan Turgenev.[105]

[Writing *Clara Milich* was a consolation to Turgenev in his illness and created a further link with Savina. In the next letter he refers to her offer to obtain a photograph of Yevlagiya Pavlovna Kadmina, the singer and actress who was the prototype of the eponymous heroine of *Clara Milich*. She committed suicide by poisoning herself during a performance in Kharkov in 1881. By a coincidence, another Russian actress killed herself about the time Turgenev finished the novel and he refers to her in this letter. She was J. N. Feigina, who had been acting at the *Comédie Française*. The cause of her suicide was her unhappiness over a nephew of Napoleon III, the Duc de Morni, whose mistress she had been and who had treated her badly.

The last lines of *Rozmova*, referred to in the previous letter, are used (inaccurately) in the thoughts of Aratov, the hero of *Clara Milich*, shortly before his death.]

(Bougival, 29 September 1882)
Dear Marya Gavrilovna,

I have just received your letter, and I want first to thank you for the kindness which you have shown to the young woman Vasilenko. I passed on the contents of your letter to Mme Viardot, who will let her know. As for your début, take comfort. If you were not capable of such nervous excitement, you would not be the person you are. I am confident that you acted excellently on Sunday and that your health was fully restored: the reserves which you built up in the country could not evaporate in a single day!

Thank you for enquiring about my health. It is improving, though with the inevitable slowness of my age. Thank you also for your suggestion of getting me a photograph of Kadmina. I do not need it any longer, for the novel of which she is the heroine is finished and has already been copied out. This is the very novel which I should like to read to you, but it will probably be published before I arrive in Petersburg and you will be able to read it in the *European Herald*. In the December issue of the *European Herald* you will also be able to read about fifty of those *Poems in Prose* from which I read two or three at Spasskoye. *But the ones I read to you will not be published.* They are completely omitted, since they are too personal. All *personal* pieces are excluded altogether. For the present, all this is a secret, so say nothing about it.

Feigina's suicide was not unexpected. She was one of those ambitious and energetic people who cannot lay claim to all that their ability deserves. This they cannot bear, especially if they suffer setbacks in such sensational circumstances. In addition she probably had a cold temperament and her pride was aroused—especially by the thought that she—Feigina!—had trodden of her own free will the path travelled by vulgar courtesans. She fancied herself immeasurably superior, and she was entitled to do so. Add to this the ease with which Russians make up their minds to commit suicide. All the same, I'm very sorry for her. And she had no premonition of the kind of maelstrom in which she found herself, with all that publicity in *Figaro* and so on. To kill oneself for the sake of such a stupid, vile creature, pour un gommeux, pour un crevé —no one could sink lower than that... and yet, no, the baseness was in giving oneself to such a loathsome creature just for the sake of money. Suicide offers the only way out, even an atonement.

I am going to stay here for another six weeks. I suppose that I shall work. And when shall I see you? Only the gods know that. Keep well and cheerful—and don't leave me without letters from you—whether or not they bear a coat-of-arms. You know, I love you very, very much. Adieu. I kiss all of you. "All?" you will ask. "Yes, all," I repeat. And then I will kiss your dear hands.

Yours, Ivan Turgenev.[106]

[The mention of a "coat-of-arms" refers to Savina's new stationery marked with the Vsevolozhsky family crest. The "début" was Savina's appearance on 24 September in *The Guilty One* by Potekhin. A critic reported that the theatre was crowded and that she, with the principal actors Davydov and Lensky, was much applauded. Yet she was not having an easy time in her career. On 29 November *New Time* carried the following item:

"It is rumoured that Madame Savina intends to retire ... It is known that Madame Savina earns 12,000 roubles a year, on the understanding that she acts twice weekly; for each additional performance she receives 200 roubles. Since her repertoire is large, she has until recently been acting three or four times a week, which should have raised her annual income to 20,000 roubles. The management have exercised their undoubted right to pass on her parts to other actresses as well and have given an invitation to Madame Ilyinskaya. Madame Savina did not remain idle on her own behalf. She demanded a benefit performance, which would have made her previous earnings up to 20,000 roubles. In all probability, the management will satisfy her wish and the 'Savina incident' will be closed—to the benefit of Russia."[107]

These were the "troubles" mentioned in Turgenev's next letter to her.]

(Bougival, 5 November 1882)

Now at last you have remembered me, dear Marya Gavrilovna! I was just beginning to think—not so much that you had completely forgotten me—but that various circumstances and preoccupations had pushed your old friend into third, or even fourth, place. But, thank goodness, I see that you have kept your old regard for me—and that makes me glad. What does not please me, however, are the petty troubles which seem to have enmeshed you when you returned to Petersburg —to the "arena of your activities", speaking portentously.

What in the world is this about? You even spoke of retiring! And what about all those new parts in which I want to see you when, if fate so wills it, I return to Petersburg? I am sure that all this was only a momentary burst of annoyance and that no trace of it remains. You must remain on the stage until the time when, with your unique talent, you can play the parts of "noble old ladies". And that means for another forty years, which of course I shall not see—a fact which I do not greatly regret.

But your news of Potekhin astonished me. What is this? Has this milksop with the ingratiating manner, this namby-pamby, really turned into a high official, a general—and one of the old school at that? Is it possible to make any assessment of people and prejudge them? It seemed likely that he would let everything go to pieces, and instead he has started to pull them together! Marvels indeed—but enough of this.

[A. A. Potekhin, brother of the dramatist, had been appointed director of the Alexandrinsky Theatre. In her notes on subsequent seasons, Savina recorded that he was totally lacking in talent for stage direction.]

I am still here; however, in about ten days I shall be returning to Paris. My condition is unchanged. I should be fine, except for the fact that I still cannot stand or walk without causing almost unbearable pains in the left side of my chest. By the way, in four days' time I shall be sixty-four, so I seem to have no right to be demanding. I must be grateful that I have not gone blind, that I still have the use of my legs, and so forth. I have become humble, dear Marya Gavrilovna, very humble. So much so, that when I recollect even last year's antics at Spasskoye, I ask myself—was it really *I*, that grey-haired but still young man who could be set on fire by one kiss from delightful lips? All this has been deposited in the archives of memory—where, by the way, this particular memory has first place and is kept on the very best shelf.

You write of your ailments, but I hope that this too is a cloud which has gathered and then lifted. I want to see you blossoming, gay, cheerful—all of which you probably are.

Well, au revoir nevertheless. Thank you for the kind things you have said; and in answer I permit myself to kiss your dear hands all over with special tenderness.

Yours, Ivan Turgenev.[108]

(Bougival, 10 November 1882) [The day after Turgenev's birthday.]

My little dove with blue wings, thank you for yesterday's telegram of congratulations. I was very moved by the fact that you remembered me.

I kiss your little hands a thousand times—I ought to say, "your little paws", and that would include your little feet as well.

Yours, Ivan Turgenev.[109]

[Savina had a slight accident; the *New Time* reported: "Today during a rehearsal, Mme Savina missed the chair as she sat down, fell, and hurt her hand." Turgenev was concerned, in spite of his own suffering at the time. He was also keeping abreast of other theatre news as his reference to Potekhin shows. Savina's marginal note on this letter confirms that he meant the play *Tormentors of Love*. A reviewer in *The Voice* wrote of it: "Potekhin has written...a long...and boring play. It was planned to stage it with Mme Savina in the main rôle; but, after careful thought, the talented actress declined to act in it."]

(Bougival, 17 November 1882)

What do I read in the papers, dear Marya Gavrilovna? You fell on the stage and hurt your hand—it is rumoured that you dislocated it. Do reassure me by writing as soon as possible—or ask somebody to write if it is the right hand that you have hurt. I seem to remember that the very same thing happened to you two years ago. I saw you in bed: you were being treated by a most unpleasant Armenian doctor. We can assume that you could not have any other kind of disaster on the stage! But even one like this—oh, that's bad!

Make sure that I get at least a line from you, and address it to Paris, 50 Rue de Douai. I am moving to Paris tomorrow, sooner than I had thought. Recently my health seems to be somewhat improved. If this improvement continues, then perhaps our meeting in Petersburg, which you so kindly mentioned in your telegram, may come about. How happy I shall be to see you! My dear, I love you very much.

I was pleased to see that you did not have a part in the play by Potekhin, which has had a bad reception. It is said that A. Potekhin, blinded by brotherly love, produced with great splendour this work by his mediocre brother. It would be a good thing if he learned a lesson from it—or if this failure deflated his bureaucratic arrogance.

In taking leave, I kiss your bad hand carefully, and the other very warmly—and everything which you do not forbid me. Do let me know about yourself.

Yours, Ivan Turgenev.[110]

(Paris, 9 December 1882)
Dear Marya Gavrilovna,

I have been intending all this time to reply to your last letter, and then suddenly I read in *The Voice*, "Mme Savina has *again* fallen ill". I was greatly distressed by this and took up my pen at once—as if that could help you! I should like to believe that this is something of a diplomatic illness—an expression of your annoyance about those theatrical affairs of which you wrote to me and which make you think of retiring! Please resolve my uncertainty. I think of you very often—and you well know in what way, with what warm, tender feelings.

As for myself, I am still in the same state—fit as a fiddle but condemned to immobility, for I can neither stand nor walk! The prospect of our meeting in Petersburg is more and more veiled in mist. I can say, with more justification than you, that I do not know what will happen to me or when I shall see you. That is why it is not very pleasant for me to think about this enigmatic future. And yet, the devil can play all kinds of tricks—or so I should say if I could believe that even the devil intervenes in human affairs. But he imitates his master and leaves these things to run as they will. For all this, I neither lose hope nor wish to lose it.

By the time you get this letter you will have in your hands my *Poems in Prose*. I wonder what you will think of them. My novel will be published in the January issue of the *European Herald* and I believe that this is the work you will prefer.

I kiss your dear hands and remain for ever,
Your old friend Turgenev.[111]

[As usual, Turgenev minimized his own illness in his concern for Savina; it was in fact the *New Time* not *The Voice* which carried the report. He gave a truer picture of his condition to the Polonskys:]

(Paris, 14 December 1882—to the Polonskys)
...It is only when I get your letters that I think of my illness, of any improvement and so on. I have come to terms with my condition and often simply hope that it will not change. Tyutchev's line can be applied to me: "The day has passed, and God be thanked for it".[112]

[He underwent a major operation early in January, with less faith in the outcome than his friends professed to feel.]

(Paris, 23 January 1883—to Madame Polonskaya)
...In a week's time I shall be quite well; and as it has now been decided that I shall be able to stand and walk and even to dance, there is nothing more to be wished for. And, of course, if I do not get to Russia it will be entirely due to my perversity![113]

[A later letter to Polonsky emphasizes the irony of the last sentence—"When you are in Spasskoye, give my greetings to the house, the garden, my young oak—and to my country that I shall probably never see again!"]

(Paris, 25 January 1883) [Written in pencil]
Dear Marya Gavrilovna,
I am still in bed after my operation. However, I hope to get up in about five days. The cut is a very large one. But I do not want to delay any longer in writing, even though I have to do it in an uncomfortable position. First of all, to thank you for your telegram of greetings; secondly to congratulate you on

your triumph in Ostrovsky's new comedy *The Handsome Male*; thirdly to persuade you to send me a line about yourself—you have been very stingy with your lines lately.

I kiss your dear hands and wish you everything that you would wish yourself.

Yours, Ivan Turgenev.[114]

(Paris, 8 February 1883—to Madame Polonskaya)

... My health has finally deteriorated. It is no longer only the collar-bone that hurts: the whole of my back and chest hurt constantly. I cannot move, and I can sleep only with injections of morphia. The nights are especially cruel...[115]

(Paris, 22 February 1883—to the same)

... I shall probably be moved to Bougival as soon as it gets warmer. It is now completely pointless to think about the future. I shall send you another bulletin in a week's time; perhaps it will be more cheerful.[116]

(Paris, 22 February 1883) [The last letter to Savina—written in pencil]

Dear Marya Gavrilovna,

Although I had the right to suppose that you would not forget me just because I have become a feeble old man (I'm writing to you in bed) I was evidently mistaken. It certainly seems, judging from the newspapers, that you have had so much on your hands lately that there has been no time to think of writing letters. I rejoice at your success from afar. But today my main purpose in writing is to find out whether you have received from Stasyulevich a copy of the *Poems in Prose* and of the novel *Clara Milich*. I entrusted this task to him.

It is, of course, senseless to think of my going to Russia. If fate wills that we should meet, it can be nowhere but here. At all events, I wish you happiness and good health with all my heart. I do not change in my affections—and I shall keep exactly the same feeling for you until the end.

Your sincerely devoted Ivan Turgenev.[117]

[After months of extreme pain, Turgenev died on 22 August 1883. Koni wrote to Savina five days later:]

On the death of anyone who is dear to us, who roused the best in our hearts, who illuminated and sanctified a great deal in our lives, our thoughts inevitably turn to those who were themselves dear to him, whom he loved, who comforted and sometimes inspired him. And these living witnesses of his feelings and his thoughts become particularly dear, particularly close to the heart which has just suffered loss. So you will understand that I want to write to Savina when my heart is burdened with the thought that Turgenev is no more.

No more—what a searing phrase! It is absurd to say that he is no more as a writer, as an artist. He has completed his task, he has moulded himself in bronze: and in that sense he is immortal as long as there is a Russian people, as long as European culture endures. But there is another feeling which is inseparably linked with the life of an outstanding public figure of whom it could also be said, "He was a man". You, of course, have experienced this feeling many times. When you created true dramatic characters (like the mayor's daughter) and felt that those around *could not* understand you, could not comprehend all the subtlety of your acting, the full depth of your insight; when at times you lost heart, surrounded as you were by smug ignorance, scheming mediocrity, all-pervading trite commonplaces—did you not then say to yourself, "He would understand, he would judge truly, he would share the inmost joy of my creation"? And would not your thoughts turn to that majestic grey head, that unforgettable figure? You did not greatly mind that he was not near you, that he was far away. There was comfort and satisfaction in the simple fact that *somewhere* there was Turgenev, that he existed.

And now he is *nowhere*! I just cannot reconcile myself to it, being a simple departmental official, a simple reader. What then must you feel, his comrade in the service of the arts—a comrade, and a dearly beloved friend as well, who was given the command, "Halt!" Alas, why can we not utter that tender word of command? Why was it not possible, if he was already destined to leave us, to stretch out our hands to him in his alien land and say, "Come to us"? What a bitter fate for Russia—to lose her best sons in this way! Take care, for you too are divinely anointed and the sacred fire of creativity burns on your brow—you were a friend to *him*. Look after yourself, conserve your strength, keep yourself strong for many years to come, so that at last you may "as a dear old lady sing your friend's song quietly at the fireside" and remain the living legend of our great man of letters.

Yours with all my heart,
A. Koni.[118]

[The quality of Koni's feeling and its expression belie his modest description of himself as a "simple departmental official". In his last sentence he may have been alluding to Ronsard's sonnet, "Quand vous serez bien vieille, au soir à la chandelle". He had a wide knowledge of European literatures and was fond of quoting from memory, not always with perfect accuracy.

Savina had spent the summer at Siva, working on the memoirs which she never completed. She returned to Petersburg on 29 August and wrote at once to Koni:]

My return to Petersburg is for no joyful occasion, Anatolii Fedorovich! People everywhere are saying, "This has been expected for a long time." I too expected it—and yet I do not believe it. I cannot—I do not want to believe it. For some reason it seemed to me that he would return home to die—just to die—and that I would see him once more at Spasskoye, his beloved Spasskoye. I hoped so earnestly, I felt so sure of it.

You are the first to whom I have spoken about him: you understand, you have remembered me—and you will understand everything. I do not even thank you for your letter—just now I can do nothing. I do not weep, I have no way of expressing my grief. This is a harder role than that of Marya Antonovna and at present I have no audience whatever. *He* is no more—not even the *he* who was far away. Everything that I hear or read these days seems so paltry and insignificant—and what is the purpose of it all? This is no egoism on my part. There may well be some who feel my loss more deeply, but to me it all seems inadequate.

I have the sense of having gone partly blind or having fallen into a lethargic sleep. I can hear and be aware, but I cannot call out. All last night I read again the dear letters of the last four years of his life. I am about to go to evening prayers, where I shall pray to the One in whom *he* did not believe. I have never before lost anyone near and dear to me, so I have not felt the comfort of prayer. Now I cannot even imagine what I shall pray for.

Inquisitive glances, trite questions, even sympathy—why are things like this insulting when they relate to him? Please come back soon: you will be able to explain.[119]

(Petersburg, 30 August 1883—Savina to Koni)

So very many thanks, dear Anatolii Fedorovich. Today I went to Matins early (so as not to meet anyone) at the monastery church (Lavra); and at last I was able to cry. I am now lying down. My head is hurting, but I feel easier....[120]

(Petersburg, 5 September 1883—Savina to Koni)

... Tonight I have a rehearsal, but should be free towards

10 o'clock. Do come, if it is not too late for you—I shall give you tea and we will talk about dear Ivan Sergeyevich....[121]

(Petersburg, 9 September 1883—Savina to Koni)
... I have heard from a reliable source that there will not be a public subscription towards the funeral, so I have sent money to the memorial fund.[122]

[The city of Petersburg bore the cost of Turgenev's funeral. His body started on the long journey from France to Russia on 2 October, when a ceremony of farewell was held at the Gare du Nord in Paris. The scene as described by eyewitnesses is taken from *Literaturnoye nasledstvo*—Literary Heritage, vol. 76, 1967:
"An improvised mortuary chapel was set up in one of the large station warehouses, the normally dreary atmosphere of which was dispelled by twelve crystal chandeliers each bearing sixteen thick wax candles. The ceremony, admission to which was by ticket, was attended by four hundred people including French writers and thinkers such as Zola, Renan and Daudet.
"With the coffin went the cap and gown which Turgenev had received on the conferment of an honorary degree at Oxford and also the famous Pushkin ring which had been used to seal the letter to Savina from Spasskoye on 29 May 1880 [see p. 50]. The carriage which bore the coffin resembled a sort of field-chapel. The walls were covered with black cloth on which hung many wreaths. A white sash with the inscription in gold 'Les Frênes'—the name of the villa where he had died—was draped over the coffin. At the head was a huge green wreath from 'La famille Viardot'. Masses of fresh flowers filled the carriage. One of Pauline Viardot's daughters —Mme Chamerot—and her husband travelled to Russia for the funeral.
"The funeral procession in Petersburg drew an even greater

crowd than that of Dostoyevsky—it was estimated as 400,000."]

(Petersburg, 11 September 1883—Savina to Koni)
... How beautifully you have expressed it: a vigil to the memory of Ivan Sergeyevich—it is the only way of describing our evening together. Yesterday I was in the Kazan cathedral and naturally could not help weeping. I stood at the back of the crowd, heavily veiled, and no one but Toporov could have seen me—and yet someone found it necessary to write in the papers about my distress. Surely this oversteps the bounds of my activity as an artist. Does an actress always and everywhere belong to the public? I have decided not to attend the funeral. Not because I want to spare my tears, but in order to give no grounds for suspicion of insincerity which would insult the memory of the dear departed. I have thought of a way to say farewell to him—and I shall do it by any means, even the impossible.[123]

(Petersburg, 11 September 1883—Koni to Savina)
You did right not to send me the letter which you were contemplating, dear Marya Gavrilovna. It would not have accorded with "the facts of the case", as our public officials would put it. On that evening, so dear to me, when we held a vigil to the memory of Ivan Sergeyevich, it was you who performed the solemn rites, while I was only a simple, devout worshipper.
But I am concerned and also worried about your idea of leaving the theatre (for to leave the Petersburg or Moscow stage is, for someone with your talent, equivalent to leaving the theatre altogether). Do you know what Paul says in his Epistle to the Colossians—"Stay, brothers, and uphold the faith!" That is what I am saying to you. Savina is not the name of an individual, but rather a collective name which stands for the very best traditions and skills combined with talent and

intelligence. You are a school of acting in yourself, and you must stand like a soldier to hold the breach which has been driven into the world of art by the absurd minions of the ridiculous baron. When the Gauls took Rome and burst into the city, they found the senators sitting motionless in their seats and involuntarily bowed to them. And your barbarians bow to you. My father kept among his cherished papers a ticket to a benefit performance by Asenkova. There is an air of old times and forgotten theatrical events about this ticket, but it is also a reminder of the actress who died on the battlefield despite most difficult personal and social problems. Let this ticket serve you as her commission from beyond the grave.

Your devoted A. Koni.[124]

[The "ridiculous baron" was Kister, who has already appeared in the background of the story. Koni's allusion to *Colossians* seems to be one of his imperfectly remembered quotations; he probably intended *2 Thessalonians* 2.15—"stand firm, then, brothers, and hold fast to the traditions" (N.E.B.).

As Turgenev had feared, Savina's husband Vsevolozhsky was pressing her to leave the theatre, and her own will was inclined in the same direction. Savina changed her mind about attending Turgenev's funeral and was in fact present. On the evening of that day she played her favourite role of Verotchka in *A Month in the Country* which was performed in memory of the author. In his next letter, Koni dates the occasion a day late:]

(Petersburg, 4 October 1883—Koni to Savina)
Dear Marya Gavrilovna,

I have not yet managed to thank you for the great pleasure for which I am indebted to you on the night of the 28th.

Speaking honestly, this pleasure is attributable only and solely to you—to your excellent acting, so packed with feeling and with deep and silent meaning. Your action when you put your head on the knees of your "benefactress", movingly and without words confessing that you are in love, affected me deeply and is still before me. But all this is you, Savina, you and no one else—neither the actors nor the author himself. Yes, even the author. The play is long, monotonous, entirely lacking dramatic movement. This plot—*tranchons le mot*—which depicts a woman at her "critical age" in whom *la bête* has stirred, clouding her head and setting her blood on fire, could possibly have been material for a one-act comedy or even a subtle *proverbe* with the good taste and skill of an Octave Feuillet. But, stretched to five acts, the theme grows pale and loses all significance. In all honesty, it is a lame thing, not worthy of the pen of Ivan Sergeyevich. It is essentially a novel put on the stage.

I admired your energy, having seen you in the morning at the funeral—tired and suffering. Apparently you did not stay to listen to the speeches at the graveside—lectures on astronomy and about the fact that Turgenev had been a student at Moscow University. How pale and colourless all this was. The following evening I was sad to learn from the programme that you were determined to read "The Last Meeting". You can imagine my joy when, in the first words that you spoke, I recognized the beloved lines from "Faust". Your decision to concentrate on this passage was most welcome. At the end of your reading, there seemed to emerge the moral bequest of Turgenev to the younger generation—and of course it would have been difficult, if not impossible, for this bequest to find a better executor than you. But the other readings—incidentally I left without listening to the end of Potekhin and Davydov— God Almighty! Is the Russian intelligentsia always and in everything condemned to a lack of proportion, to a poverty of expression or even of sincere feeling? Is it condemned to a kind of poverty of thought and consideration?

What is to be said about Grigorovich, who read the *Poems in Prose* with *his own words*, who read *The Old Woman* in a merry, rollicking tone, and sobbed out the gay, high-spirited *Sky-blue Kingdom* in a tearful, graveside voice? Could anyone have worse interpreted the tone and rhythm of those pearls of Turgenev's prose? And Annenkov—"Turgenev's best friend", his "counsellor and critic"—who could find nothing to relate from the whole wealth of Turgenev's life except the disagreeable tale of his pinching bread while exchanging stories and letting the poor old servant be blamed for it. Aren't the Spanish right in saying, "May God save us from our friends, for we ourselves can deal with our enemies"?

However, I am sure that you are bored with hearing my complaints, and you may be saying through your yawns, "Yes, save us from our friends!" I beg leave to save you, and sign

Your devoted A. Koni.[125]

[The occasion which caused Koni so much irritation was a Literary Evening arranged by the Committee of the Literary Fund, in honour of Turgenev. In the first part there were speeches by his friends Annenkov, Stasyulevich, Grigorovich and Weinberg; in the second part, Savina, Potekhin, Davydov and Polonsky read some of his works. Savina had intended to read "The Last Meeting" from *Poems in Prose* but later chose the letter about Verotchka's death from the story "Faust".

In the following year a bust of Turgenev, the work of Zhosefina Antonovna Polonskaya, was unveiled in the Volkovo cemetery where he was buried. Savina was abroad at the time and wrote to Koni about it:]

(Carlsbad, 21 June 1884)

The memorial to Ivan Sergeyevich was unveiled without either of us being present. According to descriptions it is beautiful and—what is more important—in good taste. I was so afraid of all sorts of inscriptions and such things...[126]

[Savina was present at another public ceremony in memory of Turgenev in 1908, about which she wrote to Molchanov, her third husband:]

... Today I went to Volkovo cemetery. There were many people, but not enough. The city authorities had arranged it all very well. Bishop Vladimir Putyata conducted the service. The grave was beautifully adorned. People made speeches, but not very good ones. I left at half-past one and perhaps someone may have said something good after I had gone...

[Weinberg, the dramatist who was a friend of both Savina and Turgenev, made a stage version of the novel *A Nest of Gentlefolk*, in which Savina played the part of Liza.]

(22 December 1893—Savina to Bazilevsky)

... *A Nest of Gentlefolk* is ready and, against all expectations, has turned out very well. Those competent to judge are delighted with the dramatization, but the original language has remained untouched with a few exceptions demanded by the dramatic form. What would Ivan Sergeyevich have said about it? He would have been pleased. He always wanted to write a part for me and in his actual work he portrayed me in Liza, Yelena, and especially in *Asya*. The acting will be good, with the exception of the wife's part, which there is literally no one to play but myself: but this is unthinkable. Liza is so purely imagined, and the scene of leave-taking is so moving, that there were tears in everyone's eyes. Of course, everything is incomparably fuller and more beautiful in the novel. I fear that Liza might seem boring to our contemporaries, but I shall sing my swan-song for artists and aesthetes like you. I shall scarcely be able to count ten such people among my audience, mais je suis sûre de mon fait. Turgenev is—first and foremost—music in literature. And although not everyone likes symphony orchestras, nevertheless people do not refuse to listen to them...[127]

[Savina was indulging her fancy when she identified herself with some of Turgenev's characters. *A Nest of Gentlefolk* was written in 1858 and *On the Eve*, in which Yelena appears, in 1860. When her benefit performance of *A Nest of Gentlefolk* was given on 25 January 1894, she was busy inviting her friends—and even influential men for whom she had no great liking, such as Suvorin, the editor of the *New Time*.]

(20 January 1894—to Bazilevsky)

... Give me pleasure, kindest Victor Ivanovich, and come on the 25th. Take it as a boring duty. I do so want you to see the play! My agitation over *A Nest of Gentlefolk* has no bounds. Everything seems to me unworthy of the memory of the dear author, and the slightest inaccuracy drives me to despair. I have no free time at all, for I am acting every night and in the mornings there are rehearsals. People drive one mad with requests for tickets.[128]

(January 1894—to Koni)

... You will understand how much I want to portray the lovely conception of Liza, and you will give me encouragement towards this difficult task. I am going through all the torments of hell since rehearsals started. Everything appears to me unworthy of the memory of Ivan Sergeyevich, and my presumption seems monstrous. One thing alone gives me a little comfort: even though I may not succeed in giving a good performance, at least the public will hear the beautiful language of Turgenev. Do not judge Weinberg too harshly: defend him if he is attacked. It is impossible to imagine how hard it was to do what he has done, and how he hesitated before "taking the plunge". I thought that I might have to act Lavretsky's wife, but Weinberg did not want to give Liza's part to anyone but me. The director gave orders that we should play in modern dress, which would have restricted us, but I shall disobey his order—the more readily since women's fashions at present have many features in common with those of the period.[129]

(January 1894—to Suvorin)

...I am sending you a ticket for my twentieth benefit performance, Alexei Sergeyevich. It's no joke—twenty years! My feelings when I see this figure are not easily described. There is a song which goes, "And I feel gay and I feel sad", or something of the kind. Shall I succeed in portraying Turgenev's Liza—and won't our down-to-earth public find her boring? Have you noticed that the "young recruits" do not know how to play the parts of "innocent girls"? To whom shall I pass on my inheritance?[130]

[Savina was not allowed to be simply the actress who could brilliantly interpret Turgenev's characters. Her known personal friendship with him brought incessant demands for his letters. She refused to release them for publication, though other sections of Turgenev's voluminous correspondence came out in print as the cult of his memory grew. In 1884 there appeared *The First Collection of Letters by Turgenev 1840–1883* published by the Literary Fund—a society in aid of needy artists and scholars. Koni was indignant about this volume and expressed his feelings in a letter to Savina soon after its publication.]

...I have often thought of you recently. Although I read that you, all sparkling with diamonds, were the great *attraction* at some charity ball, yet I could not help thinking that, amid all that splendour, amid all the bustle and the fire of admiring, curious, greedy glances—the figure of the dear giant with his grey hair arose before your eyes. Your heart would contract with sadness, thinking how the indifferent crowd had yet another opportunity to disturb his ashes and to rummage in his heart with their dirty, scandal-loving fingers.

Tell me what you thought, how you felt, in the days after you had looked through the elegantly produced volume with its title, "The First"—meaning that the cup has not been drained: there will be a second and a third—"Collection of the letters of Ivan Sergeyevich Turgenev".

You are a great Russian actress and I am a humble official, but I should like to think, to believe, that our thoughts and feelings are in some respects the same. Last night I dropped in for a short time on a very exclusive gathering where some of Turgenev's old friends were present. Many of them are offended by his letters—not so much by what he wrote, but rather by the fact that now it has all been made public. If you had only heard how they denigrated Ivan Sergeyevich.

Forgive my getting into a writing vein, but I cannot forget those days last October when we talked so much about him. I kiss the hand *that has not given up Turgenev's letters.*

Yours with all my heart, A. Koni.[131]

(18 November 1884—Savina to Koni)

...And what do you say about the letters? I suffered no less than you. We foresaw it, did we not? Yet I did not expect anything like this. Today the *Theatre World* (there really is such a paper) reproaches me for withholding "an interesting correspondence" and says that the letters "of such a man are common property", that the names of contemporaries could be indicated by initials and that I am guilty of burying talents. Just imagine what a sensation these "interesting" letters would create and how Boborykin would take them to pieces. Truly, poor Ivan Sergeyevich! I knew that I should get a letter from you about all this, and I was not mistaken. Thank you! I dare not talk about it at home—and I have no one to talk to. It seems that they do not even know at home that the letters have been published—and I hide the book . . .[132]

[Savina's loyalty did not fail as the years passed. She wrote to Koni in 1908, "I should very much like to talk to you about how I am being pestered with requests for letters by Ivan Sergeyevich, by those who are seizing the chance of the twenty-fifth anniversary of Turgenev's death. I have piously guarded these letters for twenty-five years." The next year brought more demands when the Academy of Sciences in Petersburg arranged a commemorative meeting—at which she was invited to read her reminiscences—and an exhibition. She wrote about the meeting to Molchanov, her third husband.]

(17 February 1909)
. . . For two days I was almost in tears with sorrow at feeling compelled to refuse to take part in the commemorative meeting in Turgenev's honour at the Academy of Sciences. That is when I needed you so much. You, I am sure, would have persuaded me not to refuse and would have made me aware of my right and my duty. The most distressing thing is that I fully realize that I was silly to refuse. The folly was committed quite consciously, and I felt like chopping off my fingers as I wrote. But I cannot—just cannot—do it. This would have been the first public appearance of an actor—or rather, what is more, an actress—in connection with Turgenev. I should have started the ball rolling—and in what circumstances! My natural boldness was not needed in this case, but neither was my natural modesty. I am terribly cross with myself, and I am scolding myself. The commemorative meeting has been fixed for 1 March.[133]

[She was more forthcoming over the exhibition; but she still would not part with the letters. Vladimir Ryshkov, one of the organizers, described how he approached her for help:]

... Naturally I turned to Marya Gavrilovna for advice. She fixed a day for a meeting but warned me that she was very busy and could give me only a few minutes. When we met she exclaimed, "How can one talk about Turgenev in such a short time?" As it turned out I stayed with her for over two hours.

"This is my pride," Marya Gavrilovna said, pointing to the two portrait-photographs of Turgenev. One bore the inscription, "To M. G. Savina from her sincerely devoted I. Turgenev, Paris, 1879", and the other, "To M. G. Savina in memory of our joint reading. Her sincerely devoted Iv. Turgenev, St Petersburg, 16 March, 1879".

"And you know," she continued, "when I get particularly depressed, when I feel the need to go back in memory to the beautiful past, I always stand before this very picture. This is the lake at Spasskoye; Polonsky painted it. And, can you imagine, Turgenev and Polonsky knocked together from boards a kind of bathing-hut because Zhosefina Antonovna and I felt too embarrassed to bathe otherwise."

Later she said, "I cherish Turgenev's letters as something very sacred, and I will not hand them over to you for your exhibition. I do not like such things. It would be unthinkable to bring such sacred relics into the middle of a crowd. I will just give the envelopes, so that people may believe in our correspondence. I would not part with the letters even for a second until I am dead. Here I am, remembering Ivan Sergeyevich with you, and it is agonizing that one wants to be reminded of him more and more. With all my heart, I wish your exhibition every possible success."

"You shall have your wish, Marya Gavrilovna," I replied. "In a day or two I shall be bringing from Oryol all the furniture from Turgenev's room at Spasskoye. And you will do me a great service if you will restore the room exactly as it was at Spasskoye."

Marya Gavrilovna was thrilled with this suggestion. When all the things had arrived from Oryol and I had notified her, she immediately came to join us. She excitedly arranged the furniture and was blissfully happy among those things which were so familiar to her...

When the exhibition opened there were fresh roses every day in a vase on Turgenev's table. They were from Savina.[134]

(Odessa, 20 March 1909—Savina to Bazilevsky)

...Not only have I been, but I helped to arrange the exhibition and I was hoping that you would drop in to have a look. I am very glad that you liked it—and how could one not like it? I have never seen a fuller and more interesting exhibition. But how could you have missed the morning ceremony at the Academy the week before the exhibition opened? If only you had heard Koni! Ivan Sergeyevich came to life again in his rendering. The impression of this reading is still with me.

It is a pity that this exhibition was undertaken so late and for such a short time. I rejoiced at the sight of so many young people at the readings and at the exhibition. "Turgenev has passed me by," Leonid Andreyev is said to have told a reporter. I would add—"And thank God for that."[135]

[Although she deplored the wrong sort of interest in Turgenev and would not yield his letters, Savina was jealous for Turgenev's memory and had feared that the twenty-fifth anniversary of his death would be eclipsed by the celebrations of Tolstoy's eightieth birthday. In August 1908, she was in Baden-Baden, the scene of Turgenev's novel *Smoke* (1867). With the characters of this story in her mind she wrote to

Bazilevsky on a card with a view of the Lichtenthaler Allee—
"The shade of Turgenev hovers here but I look in vain on the
benches for Litvinov or Pigasov." She wrote a letter to him
on the same day.]

(Baden-Baden, 7 August 1908)
... You have probably been to Baden-Baden at some time
or other and you will understand my delight. I am resting here
after my stay at Carlsbad and I find that there could be no
better place for the purpose. What lavishness! The air is
saturated with oxygen and all the surroundings fill you with
a holy peace ... This enchanting avenue (the Lichtenthaler)
which cuts across the whole town and plays so great a part in
Smoke, the Kurhaus which has preserved its charming, old-
world air—all this makes me feel ecstatic. And all this speaks
of Turgenev—and his shade hovers everywhere. On 22 August
twenty-five years will have passed since he died, but the date
will pass almost unnoticed, submerged in the Tolstoy celebrations. Imagine, here in the residence of Marya Maksimilyanovna
Baden there is no Russian library. I looked in vain for Turgenev,
wanting to reread *Smoke* her "on the spot", but I could find
nothing except some banned books ...[136]

[The faithful memory endured to the end; in November
1913, two years before her death, she was writing to Koni:
"You have not forgotten about the reading of the reminiscences of Ivan Sergeyevich? It is tomorrow."
What was the difficulty, the constraint in the friendship that
was so brief yet so intensely important to both of them? On
Savina's part there was ambivalence and uncertainty; awe of a
great writer mingled with her undoubted affection for the
"young man with grey hair". At the time of their acquaintance
and correspondence she was in love with Vsevolozhsky—to
say nothing of such minor flirtations as that with the "immortal

warrior" Skobolev. In all that passed, she was troubled by the anxiety and self-doubt that was her constant enemy.]

... I have something contradictory in my nature. You know, I did not believe Ivan Sergeyevich—I mean, I was doubtful...[137]

Every meeting with Ivan Sergeyevich cost me a tremendous effort. I was watching not only over my words but even over every thought, fearing his criticism. And that was because of what I had heard him say about some person or thing: I imagined that he was always laughing at everything and everybody. I was paralysed by the fear of seeming ridiculous in his eyes. Stupid girl that I then was, I did not understand how his great talent, his great mind and power of observation, made him see things larger than life; and his gift of speech gave remarkably vivid expression to his thoughts. His sketches were finished portraits which some people took for caricatures.[138]

I was a stupid girl. I simply could not understand how I could attract the attention of "our famous man".[139]

[But there was more than this: there was the problem of Turgenev himself. With the sensitivity of a woman and of an artist, Savina knew that there was a boundary which neither of them dared to pass if their relationship was to continue at all. For all his charm, his sophistication, his longing for deep and lasting affection, Turgenev did not find it easy to make personal relationships. There was happiness and suffering for him in the long association with Pauline Viardot and the briefer time with Savina. Polonsky, who knew him as well as any of his friends, analysed his character in a way that throws light on the last years when Savina meant so much to him. Savina wrote to Koni, "I have been struck by the true interpretation of Turgenev's character which Polonsky has made."]

... You ask me a very difficult question: why did Turgenev remain in France despite the fact that he continually longed to live in Russia? With his means he could have travelled to the Caucasus, to the Crimea, even to Siberia—there would have been no need to limit his horizon to the Moscow, Tombovsk or Orlov provinces. How this would have widened the boundaries of his talent for observation, how many new characters would have emerged from his pen! But fate decreed otherwise. My answer will scarcely satisfy you, but I shall be honest. And perhaps my guesses (or one of them) may prove helpful in your biography of my dead friend.

I have to confess that, deeply though I loved Ivan Sergeyevich, I never ventured to ask him about his relationship with Mme Viardot. First of all from a sense of tact, and secondly because I never deceived myself about his friendship with me. I did not consider myself his one and only friend. I believe that, if all his letters were published, it would become plainly evident that Turgenev had a great many friends who were as close to him as I was, beginning with Mme Viardot and Annenkov and ending with a person totally unknown to any of us. Moreover, I believe—or assume—that if the correspondence of Turgenev were published some kind of ironical remark or essentially good-natured caustic comment at my expense would be found somewhere in his letters. Such was the character of his mind, despite the inexhaustible kindness of his heart. Thirdly—because Ivan Sergeyevich himself did not really think too deeply about his relationship with the Viardot family and did not subject himself to a critical self-analysis on that score.

Ivan Sergeyevich was as fit and healthy in the climate of Petersburg as in Paris and suffered from gout here as much as there. When he came to Spasskoye, he felt, of course, that he was in his own real home where he could be entirely himself— he could even indulge in tobacco without fearing to be scolded for it. Here he was the host, there the eternal guest. Here he was independent, hospitable, dreaming of some way to improve the condition of his peasants; there he dared not treat a friend to a cup of tea or give him something to eat, however hungry he might be. There, when he was dying, he forgot about his school and his orphanage; here, people would have reminded him about them. What, then, were the reasons?

The first reason: Turgenev's mother, a very wicked but very clever woman, once said in annoyance to both her sons, "Each of you will be a one-woman man"—meaning that each of them would go on loving the same woman all their lives. Her elder son, Nikolai Sergeyevich, fully justified his mother's prophecy: he married a poor, ungainly governess and loved her passionately all his life. Even though he knew, or guessed, that she was unfaithful to him, he still remained under her thumb and carried out her every whim, even to his own ruin. When she died he was so stricken with grief that he withdrew to one room in the attic, became a recluse, and left his entire fortune not to his brother but to the niece of his dead wife.

Ivan Sergeyevich did not fully live up to his mother's prophecy. Although he always remained attached to one woman, he was not at all in love with her during the last ten or fifteen years of his life. That was made clear by his words when he complained to me that he was not loved by anyone, and that he envied me for being married while he had neither wife, mistress, nor a single woman in the world whom he could call his own. And it was clear in his actions too—he was continually falling in love, and making up to young girls who loved not him but his talent, were flattered not by him but by his fame, who spoiled not him, but his old age.

But I said that Ivan Sergeyevich did not fully live up to his mother's prophecy, meaning that he nevertheless partly justified it. During the whole of his life he could not forget the passion which, in his younger days, prompted him to tell me that he would not wish the slightest alteration in the face of Mme Viardot, so perfect did it seem to him.

The second reason: the most improbable and yet not impossible. Ivan Sergeyevich had been *hypnotized* for good and all—that is, his will had been subdued by a stronger will which he could not overcome. Otherwise, judge for yourself, was it not strange that he should be entirely happy and content to spend the summer at home in the country and yet say regretfully and nervously, "And what if Mme Viardot should write, Come! I shall have to go—I cannot hold back."

The third reason: as far as my understanding goes, Ivan Sergeyevich would never have been happy if he had married. A woman would cause him to lose interest in her if she did not know how to conceal from him the ordinary, prosaic side of her existence, or that trace of triviality which is not alien even to the great. Her very presence would become intolerable to him. It needed a very great intelligence to understand him and not once show him this trivial side of everyday life. There are very, very few women of this kind and probably Mme Viardot was among the few—one of those rare clever women. I suppose that was one of the main reasons for his loyalty and attachment to the family.

The fourth reason: Ivan Sergeyevich was an artist to the marrow of his bones. The aesthetic feeling was developed in him just as strongly as the ear is developed in great musicians. Mme Viardot, whom I did not have the honour of knowing, was another such artist. Just as actresses playing the parts of Lady Macbeth, or Ophelia, or a Parisian Camelia, or simply a chatty gossip, could arouse the spectator's admiration by their perfect acting—so Mme Viardot probably had the talent to act divinely and appear to anyone just as she wished to appear, not only on the stage of the theatre but also on the stage of life. Turgenev, with his particular bent of mind and character, could not help revering such a woman—of whom there are few.

The fifth reason: if Ivan Sergeyevich had fallen in love with a meek and innocent woman endowed with all feminine perfection and had discovered that he could make her suffer and submit to his will, then he would not have continued to love her long. For him to love for a long time, and to *become accustomed* to love, he needed the sort of person who would make him suffer, doubt, waver, be secretly jealous and dejected—one who, in a word, would torment him. It is not for me to say how much Mme Viardot made my dear friend suffer. I did not have the honour of knowing her.

The sixth reason: however much she may have slighted Ivan Sergeyevich, it was probably she alone who knew the secret of touching his heartstrings, his deepest melody. She alone could, by her conversation, her singing or her music, give to Ivan Sergeyevich moments of such true delight and self-enchantment that he was ready to suffer and to forget all for their sake.[140]

[Savina was, like Turgenev, an artist "to the marrow of her bones". Perhaps she treasured the feeling that he had for her and understood how easily it could be shattered by the intrusion of reality. It was better that he should be allowed the dream of what might have been, while she remained the unattainable ideal—like Ellis in *Phantoms* to whom Koni once compared her. The bitter-sweet happiness that she gave Turgenev speaks clearly in his own words. What did it all mean to her—respect, admiration, tenderness certainly—but what else? In the half-real, half-theatrical quality of their relationship, Savina found a genuine happiness that too often eluded her in her more serious relationships with men. The contentment, brief but secure, that she experienced in her single visit to Spasskoye, never faded. When she was helping Ryshkov to arrange Turgenev's furniture for the memorial exhibition in 1909, the past became for a moment the true reality:]

... "My goodness, the dear Sleep-easy!" she exclaimed as she caught sight of the famous divan of which Turgenev had apparently once said that anyone who simply lay down on it would fall asleep at once.

"How many people have sat on it, lain on it, argued on it, experienced so much on it! And, look, his guns and his drozhki! I can just see Ivan Sergeyevich getting ready for the hunt. Gentlemen, you have given me a rare pleasure, a pleasure which I had no hope of feeling again. Here you are—hard and devotedly at work. But you are toiling to honour the *memory* of a great man. For me all this is alive—do you understand? It is alive, familiar—it is my very own...."[141]

[The following material has been taken from *Turgenev i Savina*, edited by Molchanov and Koni, 1918.]

The Plan
for the Continuation of Reminiscences of M. G. Savina of I. S. Turgenev.
(A rough draft).

M. G. Savina evidently intended to continue her reminiscences of Turgenev, but she did not manage to carry out her plan. Among her notes has been preserved a notebook where she had outlined a preliminary plan of the intended work. We quote the text from this MS in its entirety.

THE PLAN
The 80-ties

Literary evening. (Joint reading).
Return from Moscow.
Second literary evening. A Lone Wolf.
Slight indisposition.
My visit—at Morskaya II. (Strepetova).
Meeting A. N. Mukhortova. (A letter).
An evening at her house.
The "Whims" of Ivan Sergeyevich.
"A cup of tea". (Invitation by letter).
A Matinée performance *The Mayor's Wife*. The gift of a book.
A sprained hand.
Passing through Oryol to Odessa with R. A. Potekhina.

A spray of lilac.

Telegrams, letters connected with the Pushkin celebrations. The speech.

Meeting Maslov.

Skobolev.

Spasskoye. 1881

The meeting in Oryol.

Travelling to Mtsensk.

Lime-trees.

Zakhar and soda water.

A spring of water.

"Voices of the night".

Mass on the wedding anniversary of the Polonskys.

Village festivities. The speech made by I.S.

A walk in the woods. (Borya).

A tale of the woman neighbour weeping for her son.

Portraits. "Sleep-easy".

Confession.

Principal names mentioned in the Text

ANDREYEV, L. 1871–1919. Playwright, representative of the metaphysical and pessimistic school of writing.
ANNENKOV, P. V. 1812–1887. Literary critic, author of a Pushkin biography and great friend of Turgenev.
BATYUSHKOV, F. D. 1857–1920. Literary historian and critic. Chairman of the Literary Society.
BAZILEVSKY, V. I. Industrialist, owner of gold mines.
BELYAYEV, Y. 1876–1917. Leading theatre critic.
BERNHARDT, SARAH. 1844–1923. French actress.
BOBORYKIN, P. D. 1836–1921. Writer.
BURENIN, V. P. 1841–1926. Poet, literary critic.
BUSCH, WILHELM. 1832–1908. German artist and nonsense writer. Famous for his comic drawings.
DOSTOYEVSKY, F. M. 1821–1881. Novelist. Author of *Crime and Punishment*, *The Brothers Karamazov* and other works.
FILOSOFOV, D. V. 1872–1940. Literary critic and publicist.
FONVIZIN, D. 1743–1792. Author of the first truly national comedy *The Minor*.
GARSHIN, V. M. 1855–1888. Writer.
GOGOL, N. V. 1809–1852. Author of the play *The Government Inspector*, the novel *Dead Souls* and other works.
GONCHAROV, I. A. 1812–1891. Novelist. Author of *Oblomov*.
GRIBOYEDOV, A. S. 1795–1829. Author of the comedy *Woe from Wit*.
GRIGOROVICH, D. V. 1822–1899. Writer.
KRYLOV, V. A. 1838–1906. Playwright. 1893–96 in charge of the Alexandrinsky Company.
MARYA MAKSIMILYANOVNA, PRINCESS. 1841–1914. Wife of Prince Wilhelm of Baden.
MASLOV, I. I. 1817–1891. Distinguished civil servant who was Head of the Department of Weights and Measures.
MEYERHOLD, V. E. 1874–. Believed to have died in 1940. Producer.
MOLCHANOV, A. E. 1856–1921. Official charged with special duties

in connection with the management of Imperial theatres. Savina's third husband.

OSTROVSKY, A. N. 1823–1886. Leading playwright.

POBEDONOSTSEV, K. P. 1827–1907. Reactionary statesman.

POLONSKAYA, Z. A. Sculptress, wife of Y. P. Polonsky.

POLONSKY, Y. P. 1829–1898. Poet and critic.

POTEKHIN, A. A. 1829–1908. Writer and playwright.

PUSHKIN, A. S. 1799–1837. Author of *Eugene Onegin*, *The Queen of Spades*, *The Captain's Daughter*, *Boris Godunov* and other works.

SAND, GEORGE. 1804–1876. French woman writer.

SHPAZHINSKY, I. V. 1844–1917. Writer.

SKOBOLEV, M. D. 1843–1882. General active in the Russo-Turkish War.

STANISLAVSKY, K. (ALEXEYEV). 1863–1938. Producer, founder of the Moscow Art Theatre.

STASYULEVICH, M. M. 1826–1911. Editor of the *European Herald* 1866–1908.

SUVORIN, A. S. 1834–1912. Journalist, publisher of the paper *New Time*.

TCHAIKOVSKY, M. I. 1850–1916. Playwright. Younger brother of P. I. Tchaikovsky.

TCHAIKOVSKY, P. I. 1840–1893. Composer.

TOLSTOY, L. N. 1828–1910. Novelist and philosopher. Author of *War and Peace*, *Anna Karenina* and many other works.

TOPOROV, A. V. 1831–1887. Turgenev's friend and agent.

TYUTCHEV, I. F. 1803–1873. Poet.

VSEVOLOZHSKY, N. N. 1846–1896. Second husband of M. G. Savina.

WEINBERG, P. I. 1831–1908. Poet and translator. Academician.

YERMOLOVA. 1853–1928. Great Russian actress.

ZHUKOVSKY, V. A. 1783–1853. Poet, translator. In 1825 he became tutor to the heir to the throne, the future Alexander II.

Alexandrinsky Theatre: since renamed the Pushkin Theatre.

Iconostasis (Russian *ikonostas*, Greek *eikonostasion*)—the screen which shuts off the sanctuary and altar from the view of the congregation in an Orthodox church. It is richly decorated with icons.

Literary Fund—a Society in aid of needy artists and scholars.

Raznochinets—intellectual not belonging to the gentry in nineteenth-century Russia.

Theatre Society—a Society for helping needy actors. It was founded on Savina's initiative in Petersburg in 1883.

Sources

1. Turgenev's letters to Savina. *Polnoye sobraniye sochinenii i pisem.* Collected Works, vols. 12 ii, 13 i and 13 ii. Leningrad 1967.

2. M. G. Savina, *Goresti i skitaniya.* My Wanderings and Tribulations. The material covers the years 1854–1877. Leningrad–Moscow 1961.

3. *Turgenev i Savina.* Turgenev and Savina. Edited by Molchanov and Koni. Petrograd 1918.

4. *Konchina Savinoi.* Savina's Death. A collection of reminiscences of Savina. The two volumes also contain speeches, letters of condolences, reports of memorial meetings. 1916–1917.

5. *Inostrannaya literatura* N I, 1971. The Journal of Foreign Literature. Recently discovered letters by I. S. Turgenev. (From the Viardot archive.)

6. Letters by P. I. Tchaikovsky covering the years 1885–86. Vol. XIII.

7. *Savina i Koni. Perepiska 1883–1915.* Correspondence between Savina and Koni. Leningrad–Moscow 1938.

8. A. F. Koni. *Sobraniye sochinenii.* Collected Works. Vol. 6. *Statyi i vospominaniya o russkikh literatorakh.* Articles about and reminiscences of Russian writers.
Vol. 8. *Pis'ma.* Letters. 1868–1927. Moscow 1968.

9. I. Shneiderman. *Marya Gavrilovna Savina.* Moscow–Leningrad 1956.

10. Y. P. Polonsky. *I. S. Turgenev at home during his last visit to Russia. Niva,* N 5, 1884.

11. M. A. Shchepkin. *I. S. Turgenev in Spasskoye-Lutovinovo. Krasny arkhiv* N 3, 1940. *Istoricheskii vestnik* 1898.

NOTE The principal source is Turgenev's correspondence, item 1 above; all material from this source is listed simply by number, referring to the editorial numbering of items in the Collected Works.

References

1. *Turgenev i Savina*. Edited by Molchanov and Koni.
2. I. S. Turgenev, Collected Works, vol. 12 ii: 4807.
3. 4818. 4. 4833. 5. 4854.
6. 4875. 7. 4934. 8. 4944.
9. 4950. 10. 4980. 11. 4997.
12. 5083. 13. 5086. 14. 5087.
15. 5088. 16. 5091. 17. 5093.
18. 5105. 19. 5122. 20. 5123.
21. 5125. 22. 5134. 23. 5138.
24. 5145. 25. 5147. 26. 5148.
27. 5154. 28. 5157. 29. 5162.
30. 5172. 31. 5175.
32. A. F. Koni, Collected Works, vol. 8.34.
33. 5180. 34. 5195. 35. 5201.
36. 5227. 37. 5234. 38. 5242.
39. 5248. 40. 5250. 41. 5290.

I. S. Turgenev, Collected Works, vol. 13 i:
42. 5316. 43. 5318. 44. 5378.
45. 5421. 46. 5430.
47. A. F. Koni, Collected works, vol. 8.46.
48. 5476.
49. *Turgenev i Savina*. Also I. Shneiderman: *Marya Gavrilovna Savina*.
50. 5477.
51. *Turgenev i Savina*. *Konchina Savinoi*, vol. 2. Shneiderman.
52. *Turgenev i Savina*. Shneiderman.
53. *Turgenev i Savina*.
54. 5493.
55. M. A. Shchepkin, *Istoricheskii vestnik*, p. 913.
56. 5500. 57. 5507. 58. 5538.
59. 5544. 60. 5554.
61. I. S. Turgenev, Collected Works, vol. 13 i, editors' note to letter 5554.

62. 5585.   63. 5591.   64. 5605.
65. 5615.   66. 5632.   67. 5674.
68. 5687.   69. 5690.   70. 5692.
71. 5693.   72. 5694.   73. 5695.
74. 5700.   75. 5697.   76. 5698.
77. 5701.   78. 5702.
79. *Turgenev i Savina.*
80. 5704.   81. 5711.   82. 5714.
83. 5715.   84. 5717.   85. 5724.
86. 5733.   87. 5734.   88. 5735.
89. 5750.   90. 5761.   91. 5773.
92. 5782.   93. *Turgenev i Savina.*
94. 5777.   95. 5794.
96. *Turgenev i Savina.*
97. 5817.   98. 5820.   99. 5833.
100. 5855.
101. I. S. Turgenev, Collected Works, vol. 13 ii: 5888.
102. 5897.   103. 5904.
104. Editors' note to letter 5904.
105. 5920.   106. 5936.
107. Editors' note to letter 5990.
108. 5990.   109. 6001.   110. 6015.
111. 6044.   112. 6049.   113. 6109.
114. 6111.   115. 6121.   116. 6128.
117. 6129.
118. A. F. Koni, Collected Works, vol. 8.23.
119. *Turgenev i Savina.*
120. *Turgenev i Savina.*
121. *Turgenev i Savina.*
122. *Turgenev i Savina.*
123. *Turgenev i Savina.*
124. A. F. Koni, Collected Works, vol. 8.24.
125. A. F. Koni, Collected Works, vol. 8.25.
126. *Turgenev i Savina.*
127. *Turgenev i Savina.*
128. *Turgenev i Savina.*
129. *Turgenev i Savina.*
130. *Turgenev i Savina.*

131. *Savina i Koni, Perepiska 1883–1915.*
132. *Turgenev i Savina.*
133. *Turgenev i Savina.*
134. *Konchina Savinoi,* vol. 2.
135. *Turgenev i Savina.*
136. *Turgenev i Savina.*
137. *Turgenev i Savina.*
138. *Turgenev i Savina.*
139. *Turgenev i Savina.*
140. *Turgenev i Savina.*
141. *Turgenev i Savina.*